— RESTRICTED —

FOR OFFICIAL USE ONLY

T. O. NO. 01-115GA-1

PT-19, PT-23 and PT-26 AIRPLANES
PILOT'S FLIGHT OPERATING INSTRUCTIONS

by United States Army Air Force

This manual is sold for historic research purposes only, as an entertainment. It is not intended to be used as part of an actual flight training program. No book can substitute for flight training by an authorized instructor. The licensing of pilots is overseen by organizations and authorities such as the FAA and CAA. Operating an aircraft without the proper license is a federal crime.

This publication contains specific instructions for pilots and should be available for Transition Flying Training as contemplated in AAF Reg. 50-16.

This publication shall not be carried in aircraft on combat missions or when there is a reasonable chance of its falling into the hands of the enemy.

Published by authority of the Commanding General, Army Air Forces, and accepted by the Air Council of the United Kingdom.

NOTICE: This document contains information affecting the national defense of the United States within the meaning of the Espionage Act, 50 U. S. C., 31 and 32, as amended. Its transmission or the revelation of its contents in any manner to an unauthorized person is prohibited by law.

©2011 PERISCOPE FILM LLC
ALL RIGHTS RESERVED
ISBN# 978-1-935700-57-9

— RESTRICTED —

10 APRIL 1943
REVISED 5 AUGUST 1944

RESTRICTED

FOR OFFICIAL USE ONLY

T. O. NO. 01-115GA-1

PILOT'S FLIGHT OPERATING INSTRUCTIONS

FOR

ARMY MODELS

PT-19, PT-19A, PT-19B
PT-23 and PT-26
AIRPLANES

This publication contains specific instructions for pilots and should be available for Transition Flying Training as contemplated in AAF Reg. 50-16.

This publication shall not be carried in aircraft on combat missions or when there is a reasonable chance of its falling into the hands of the enemy.

Published by authority of the Commanding General, Army Air Forces, and accepted by the Air Council of the United Kingdom.

NOTICE: This document contains information affecting the national defense of the United States within the meaning of the Espionage Act, 50 U. S. C., 31 and 32, as amended. Its transmission or the revelation of its contents in any manner to an unauthorized person is prohibited by law.

THIS PUBLICATION HAS BEEN
DECLASSIFIED AS REQUIRED BY
ARMY REGULATION 380-5.

RESTRICTED

10 APRIL 1943
REVISED 5 AUGUST 1944

RESTRICTED
T. O. No. 01-115GA-1

THIS PUBLICATION MAY BE USED BY PERSONNEL RENDERING SERVICE TO THE UNITED STATES OR ITS ALLIES

Instructions Applicable to AAF Personnel.

Paragraph 5.d. of Army Regulation 380-5 relative to the handling of restricted printed matter is quoted below:

"d. Dissemination of restricted matter.—The information contained in restricted documents and the essential characteristics of restricted material may be given to *any person known to be in the service of the United States and to persons of undoubted loyalty and discretion who are cooperating in Government work*, but will not be communicated to the public or to the press except by authorized military public relations agencies."

Instructions Applicable to Navy Personnel.

Navy Regulations, Article 75½, contains the following paragraphs relating to the handling of restricted matter:

"(b) *Restricted* matter may be disclosed to persons of discretion in the Government service when it appears to be in the public interest.

"(c) *Restricted* matter may be disclosed, under special circumstances, to persons not in the Government service when it appears to be in the public interest."

The Bureau of Aeronautics Circular Letter No. 12-43 further states:

"Therefore, it is requested that all naval activities check their own local regulations and procedures to make sure that handbooks, service instructions and other *restricted* technical publications are actually being made available to both civilian and enlisted personnel who have use for them."

General.

These instructions permit the issue of restricted publications to civilian contract and other accredited schools engaged in training personnel for Government work, to civilian concerns contracting for overhaul and repair of aircraft or aircraft accessories, and to similar commercial organizations.

---LIST OF REVISED PAGES ISSUED---

NOTE: A heavy black vertical line, to the left of the text on revised pages, indicates the extent of the revision. This line is omitted where more than 50 percent of the page is revised.

Page No.	Latest Revised Date
I	5 August 1944
II	5 July 1944
2	5 August 1944
11	5 August 1944
12	5 August 1944
14	5 August 1944
15	5 August 1944
16	5 August 1944
16A	5 August 1944
16B	5 August 1944
17	5 August 1944
18 Deleted	5 August 1944
24	5 August 1944
25	5 August 1944
26	5 August 1944
27	25 May 1944
28	25 May 1944
29	25 May 1944
30	25 May 1944
31	25 May 1944
32	25 May 1944
33	25 May 1944
34	25 May 1944
35	25 May 1944
36 Deleted	
38	5 August 1944

ADDITIONAL COPIES OF THIS PUBLICATION MAY BE OBTAINED AS FOLLOWS:

AAF ACTIVITIES.—Submit requisitions through the Air Inspector, Technical, whenever practicable, in accordance with T. O. No. 00-25-3 to the Commanding General, Fairfield Air Service Command, Patterson Field, Ohio. Attn: Publications Distribution Branch, as outlined in AAF Regulation 5-9. For details of Technical Order distribution, see T. O. No. 00-25-3.

NAVY ACTIVITIES.—Submit requests to the Chief, Bureau of Aeronautics, Navy Department, Washington, D. C. Also, see NavAer 00-500 for details on distribution of technical publications.

BRITISH ACTIVITIES.—Submit requirements on Form 294A, in duplicate, to the Air Publications and Forms Store, New College, Leadhall Lane, Harrogate, Yorkshire, England.

RESTRICTED   T. O. No. 01-115GA-1

TABLE OF CONTENTS

Section		Page
I	Introduction	1
II	Description	1
	1. Airplanes	1
	2. Power Plants	2
	3. Controls and Operational Equipment	4
	4. Flying Characteristics	14
III	Flight and General Operating Instructions PT-19, PT-19A, PT-19B, and PT-26	15
	1. On Entering the Cockpit	15
	2. Procedure Preliminary to Starting	15
	3. Starting	15
	4. Warm-up and Ground Test	15
	5. Taxying	16
	6. Take-off	16
	7. Engine Failure During Take-off	16A
	8. Climbing	16A
	9. Flight	16A
	10. Engine Failure During Flight	16A
	11. Approach for Landing	16A
	12. Landing	16A
	13. Emergency Take-off if Landing is not Completed	16A
	14. Stopping Engine	16B
	15. Before Leaving the Cockpit	16B

Section		Page
	16. Maneuvers Prohibited	16B
IV	Flight Operation Data	17
	1. Determining Gross Weight	17
	2. Flight Planning	17
	Weight and Balance Chart PT-19	19
	Weight and Balance Chart PT-19A	20
	Weight and Balance Chart PT-19B	21
	Weight and Balance Chart PT-23	22
	Weight and Balance Chart PT-26	23
	Specific Engine Flight Chart PT-19, PT-19A, and PT-19B	24
	Specific Engine Flight Chart PT-23	25
	Specific Engine Flight Chart PT-26	26
	Take-off, Climb and Landing Chart PT-19	27
	Take-off, Climb and Landing Chart PT-19A	28
	Take-off, Climb and Landing Chart PT-19B	29
	Take-off, Climb and Landing Chart PT-23	30
	Take-off, Climb and Landing Chart PT-26	31
	Flight Operation Instruction Chart PT-19, PT-19A	32
	Flight Operation Instruction Chart PT-19B	33
	Flight Operation Instruction Chart PT-23	34
	Flight Operation Instruction Chart PT-26	35

Appendix		Page
I	Glossary of Terms	37
II	Emergency Instructions	38
III	Extreme Weather Notes	38

Revised 5 August 1944   RESTRICTED

RESTRICTED T. O. No. 01-115GA-1

Figure 1

Figure 2

Figure 3

RESTRICTED   T. O. No. 01-115GA-1

SECTION I

INTRODUCTION

1. This Handbook describes the Operation and Flight Instructions for Models PT-19, PT-19A, PT-19B, PT-23, and PT-26 airplanes manufactured by the Fairchild Aircraft Division of the Fairchild Engine and Airplane Corporation, Hagerstown, Maryland, and the Aeronca Aircraft Corporation, Middletown, Ohio, Fleet Aircraft, Limited, Fort Erie, Ontario, Howard Aircraft Corporation, Chicago, Illinois, and St. Louis Aircraft Corporation, St. Louis Missouri.

2. While all of the subject models are similar in appearance, the equipment of each differs as explained in the text. When no mention is made of any differences, the instructions given include all models. Each paragraph which contains description or instructions applicable only to certain models is headed by the models to which it specifically refers.

3. In some cases one particular airplane may not conform exactly to the description given of it in this Handbook. The reason for this is that the Handbook has been written to cover the majority of airplanes built, and changes in various models occur from time to time which cannot always be anticipated. For example, the PT-23 airplane was designed to use an oil dilution system. The first few PT-23 airplanes were not equipped with an oil dilution system because of various shortages which made it impossible at the time of production. It is expected that the oil dilution system will be installed in these airplanes in the field when the parts become available.

SECTION II

DESCRIPTION

1. AIRPLANES.

    a. GENERAL. - Models PT-19, PT-19A, PT-19B, PT-23, and PT-26 are identical in primary design and construction. All are cantilever low-wing monoplanes with fabric-covered welded steel tube fuselage, fixed landing gear, plywood-covered wood center section and outer wing panels. All are two-place with tandem seating arrangement. The PT-26 is equipped with an enclosure over both cockpits. Other models are open cockpit. Power plants are as follows:

Figure 4 - Model PT-26 Canopy Latch

PT-19, PT-19A, and PT-19B	Ranger L-440-1	175 hp
PT-23	Continental R-670-4	220 hp
PT-26	Ranger L-440-3	200 hp

    b. ACCESS TO AIRPLANES. - A walkway on the center section on the left side of the airplane is provided on the PT-19. All other models have walkways on both sides. The enclosure on the PT-26 is opened by lifting the trip lever (figure 4) which extends outside the enclosure frame. A handhole is provided on the left side of the fuselage to assist in entering the airplane.

c. FUEL AND OIL.

(1) FUEL.

(a) PT-19, PT-19A, PT-19B ONLY. - Seventy-three octane fuel should be used. Sixty-two octane may be used in emergency.

(b) PT-23 ONLY. - Seventy-three octane fuel must be used.

(c) PT-26 ONLY. - Ninty-one octane fuel should be used by fuel between 80 and 91 octane may be used if necessary.

(2) OIL (ALL MODELS).

(a) For normal operation an oil of SAE viscosity 60 is used. Specification No. AN-VV-O-446, grade 1120.

(b) In extreme cold weather SAE viscosity 50 is used. Specification No. AN-VV-O-446, Grade 1100.

d. EMERGENCY EQUIPMENT. - A hand-type fire extinguisher is located on the rear of the fire wall, accessible from the front cockpit or through the door marked "Fire Extinguisher" in the left fuselage cowl just above and forward of the leading edge of the center section. (See figure 5.) A welded steel turnover structure is provided between both cockpits to prevent injury to occupants in event of nose-over. No special emergency exits are provided. On the PT-26, occupants should open the enclosure fully in the normal manner by grasping the handle and trip lever and sliding enclosure section to "FULL-OPEN" position.

CAUTION DO NOT USE THE FIRE EXTINGUISHER INSIDE COCKPIT DURING FLIGHT WITHOUT FIRST OPENING THE ENCLOSURE (PT-26).

2. POWER PLANTS.

a. PT-19, PT-19A, AND PT-19B. - These are powered by the Ranger L-440-1 six-cylinder in-line air-cooled engine driving a two-bladed fixed pitch wood propeller, Sensenich model 86-R-61 mounted on a Warner hub, model 7900. This engine has a compression ratio of 6:1 and is rated at 175 horse power at 2450 rpm at sea level.

b. PT-23. - This is powered by the Continental R-670-4 seven-cylinder radial air-cooled engine driving a two-bladed fixed pitch wood propeller, Sensenich

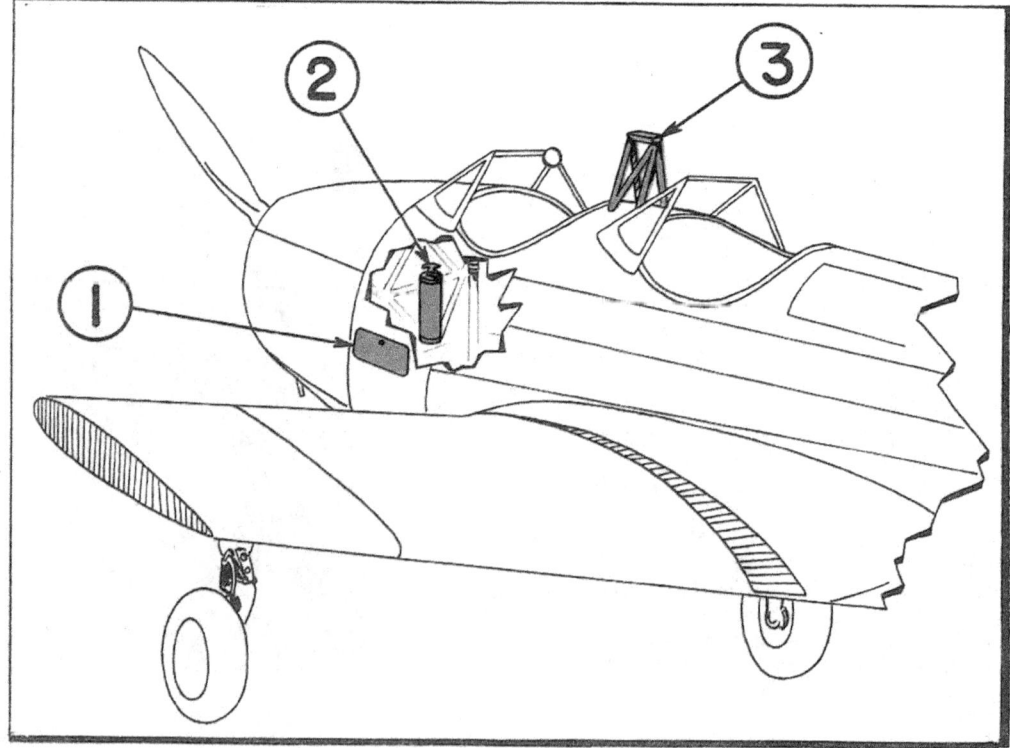

Figure 5 - Emergency Equipment - All Models

1. FIRE EXTINGUISHER DOOR
2. FIRE EXTINGUISHER
3. TURN OVER STRUCTURE

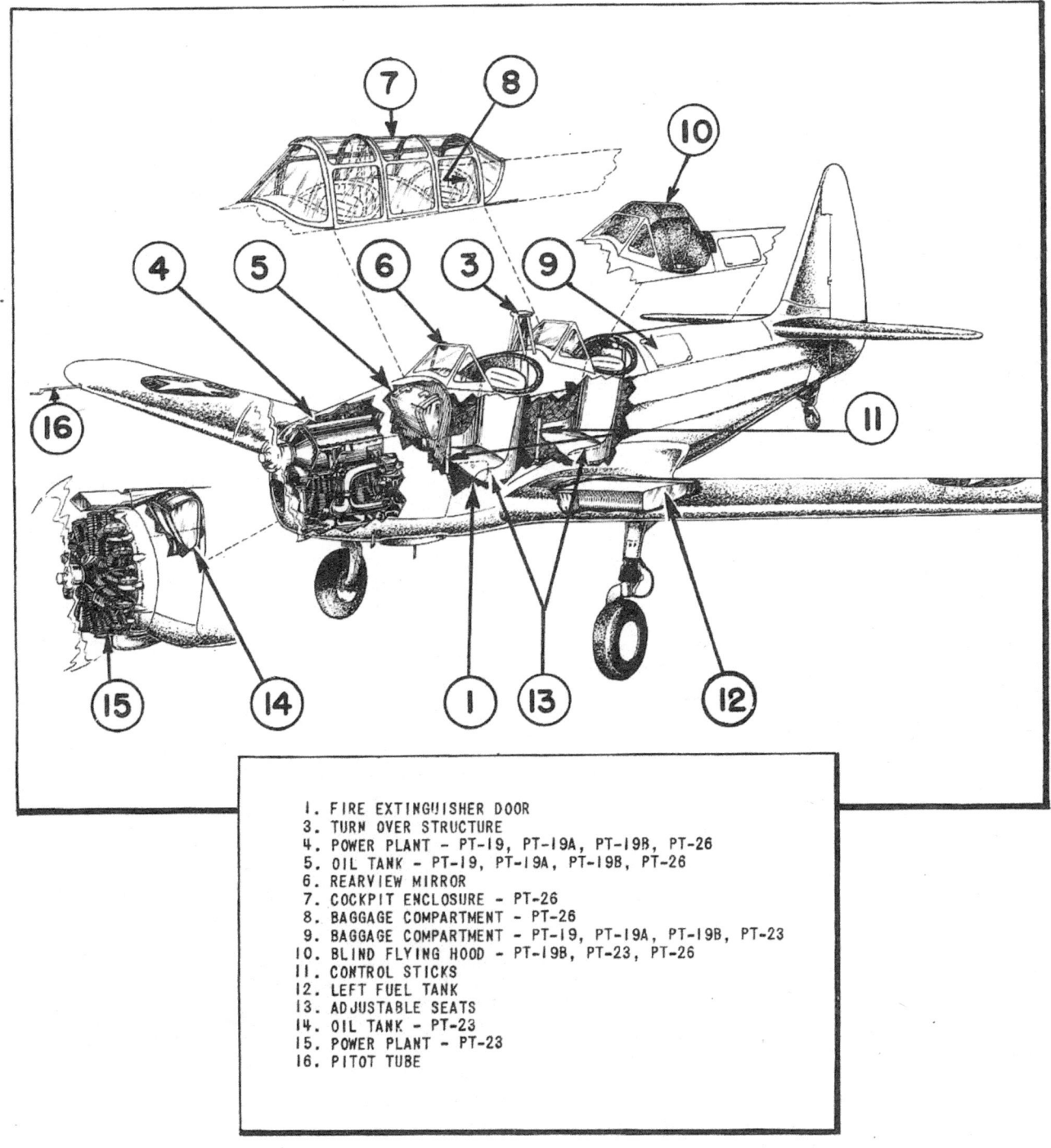

Figure 6 - Fuselage Contents Arrangement - All Models

1. FIRE EXTINGUISHER DOOR
3. TURN OVER STRUCTURE
4. POWER PLANT - PT-19, PT-19A, PT-19B, PT-26
5. OIL TANK - PT-19, PT-19A, PT-19B, PT-26
6. REARVIEW MIRROR
7. COCKPIT ENCLOSURE - PT-26
8. BAGGAGE COMPARTMENT - PT-26
9. BAGGAGE COMPARTMENT - PT-19, PT-19A, PT-19B, PT-23
10. BLIND FLYING HOOD - PT-19B, PT-23, PT-26
11. CONTROL STICKS
12. LEFT FUEL TANK
13. ADJUSTABLE SEATS
14. OIL TANK - PT-23
15. POWER PLANT - PT-23
16. PITOT TUBE

model 90-LA-77 mounted on a 98-29524B hub. This engine has a compression ratio of 5.4:1 and is rated at 220 horse power at 2075 rpm at sea level.

c. PT-26. - This is powered by the Ranger L-440-3 six-cylinder in-line air-cooled engine driving a two-bladed fixed pitch wood propeller, Sensenich model 86-R-61 mounted on a Warner hub, model 7900. This engine has a compression ratio of 7.5:1 and is rated at 200 horse power at 2450 rpm at sea level.

RESTRICTED   T. O. No. 01-115GA-1

3. CONTROLS AND OPERATIONAL EQUIPMENT.

   a. AIRPLANE CONTROLS.

   (1) COCKPIT SEATS. - Seats are adjustable. Adjustment is accomplished by lifting handle on right side of seat and sliding up or down to desired position, then the handle is released.

   (2) AILERON AND ELEVATOR. - Conventional dual stick control is provided. Either stick may be removed by removal of a single bolt through socket at bottom of stick. Controls are push-pull rod type with ball-bearing rod ends.

   (3) RUDDER, BRAKES, AND TAIL WHEEL. - Rudder and tail wheel operate together through a single system of push-pull rods with ball-bearing rod ends. A spring-loaded rod operates the tail wheel steering mechanism from the right rudder horn. Tail wheel is steerable up to the extreme positions of rudder travel and automatic full swivel beyond these positions. Rudder pedals may be adjusted by use of the lever extending upward on the inside of the pedal quadrants. Three different positions are available. After adjusting pedals, make certain that left and right pedals are in the same position. The hydraulic brakes are operated by depressing the toe pedals.

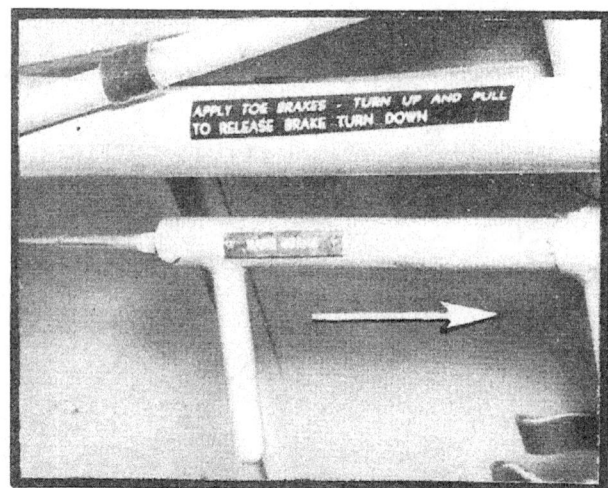

Figure 8 - Parking Brake - Front Cockpit

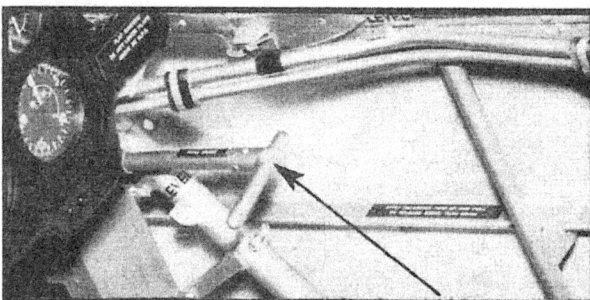

Figure 9 - Parking Brake - Rear Cockpit

Figure 7 - Rudder Pedal Adjustment Levers

   PARKING BRAKE. - The parking brake is operated by a lever on the right side of either cockpit. Depress toe brakes, move parking brake lever up and aft as far as it will go and then move it down. This holds the pressure in the hydraulic brake system. To release, depress toe brakes and return lever to "OFF" position.

CAUTION

BE SURE TO CHECK PARKING BRAKE FOR "OFF" POSITION BEFORE ATTEMPTING TO TAXI.

   (4) ELEVATOR TABS. - A tab control unit is located on the left side of each cockpit. Each is interconnected with the other. The handle is rotated clockwise, as viewed from the face for "Nose-Down" adjustment and counterclockwise for "Nose-Up."

Figure 10 - Tab Control

   (5) FLAP CONTROLS. - Flaps are adjusted by means of the lever on the left side of either cockpit. The lever is moved all the way back and released at last notch for "FULL-DOWN" position. Reverse procedure is followed to move flaps "up." Flaps may be adjusted to "HALF-DOWN" position by releasing the lever so it locks in the middle notch.

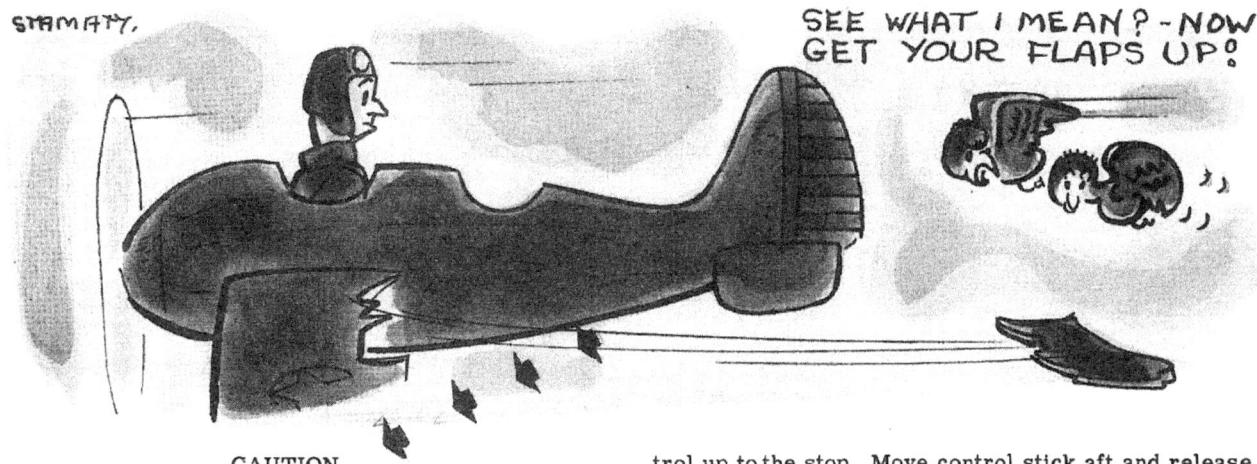

CAUTION

DO NOT LOWER FLAPS WHEN INDICATED AIR SPEED EXCEEDS 95 MPH.

(6) SURFACE CONTROL LOCK. - This system consists of a latch, holding the control sticks in full forward centered position, and a pair of cams which lock the rudder pedals in neutral position. The latch and cams are interconnected.

(a) FRONT COCKPIT OPERATION. - Move the lock handle to rear position. Center rudder pedals and release all pressure from pedals. Move stick forward into socket of latch. To unlock, move stick slightly forward and remove the latch from the stick.

Figure 11 - Wobble Pump and Flap Control
17. WOBBLE PUMP   18. FLAP LEVER

(b) REAR COCKPIT OPERATION. - Pull wire control up to the stop. Center rudder pedals and release all pressure from pedals. Center stick and move it to full forward position. Release the wire pull. To unlock, move stick slightly forward and pull wire control up to the stop. Move control stick aft and release wire pull.

CAUTION

NO PRESSURE SHOULD BE APPLIED TO THE RUDDER PEDALS WHILE OPERATING THE LOCK.

RESTRICTED   T. O. No. 01-115GA-1

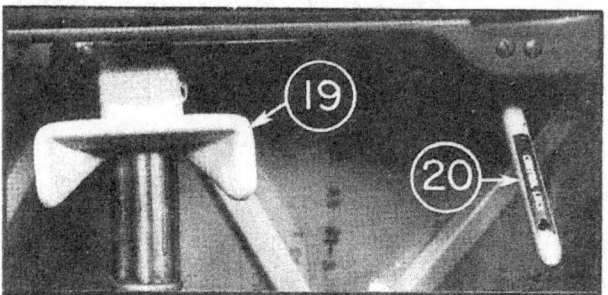

Figure 12 - Control Lock - Front Cockpit
19. STICK LATCH   20. LOCK HANDLE

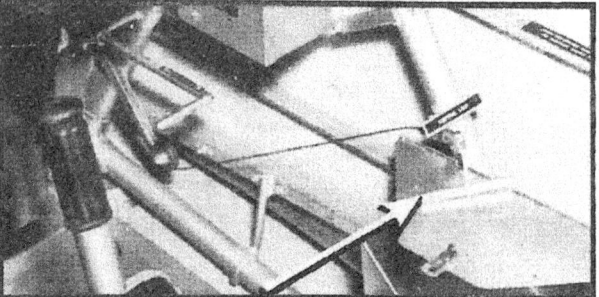

Figure 13 - Control Lock - Rear Cockpit

21. AIRSPEED INDICATOR
22. COMPASS
    PT-19, PT-19A -
    FRONT COCKPIT ONLY
    PT-19B, PT-23 -
    REAR COCKPIT ONLY
    PT-26 - BOTH
    COCKPITS
23. ENGINE GAGE UNIT
24. TACHOMETER
25. PT-19, PT-19A -
    FRONT COCKPIT ONLY
    PT-19B, PT-23 -
    BOTH COCKPITS
    PT-26 - REAR COCKPIT
    ONLY
26. ALTIMETER
27. CARBURETOR AIR HEAT
    CONTROL
28. INSTRUMENT LIGHT
    SWITCH AND RHEOSTAT
29. NAVIGATION LIGHT
    SWITCH
30. TURN AND BANK
    INDICATOR
31. RATE OF CLIMB
    INDICATOR
32. VOLTAGE BOOSTER
    (INVERTER) SWITCH
33. GYRO HORIZON
34. LANDING LIGHT
    SWITCH
35. GENERATOR BRAKE
    CONTROL PT-26 -
    FRONT COCKPIT ONLY
36. AMMETER
    PT-26 - FRONT
    COCKPIT ONLY
37. DIRECTIONAL GYRO
38. SUCTION GAGE
39. OIL DILUTION SWITCH
40. TAIL LIGHT SWITCH
41. COCKPIT HEATER
    CONTROL
42. WING LIGHTS SWITCH

Figure 14 - PT-19, PT-19A Instrument Panel

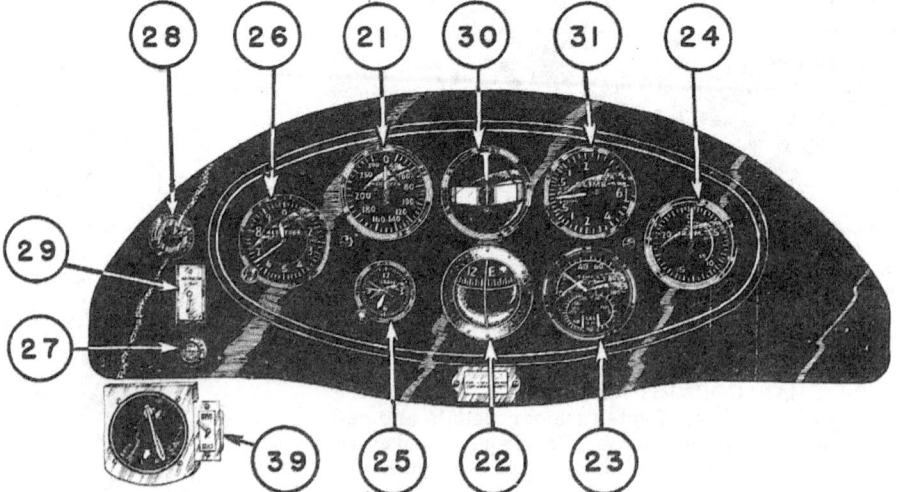

Figure 15 - PT-19B, PT-23, Instrument Panel

- 6 -

RESTRICTED

RESTRICTED   T. O. No. 01-115GA-1

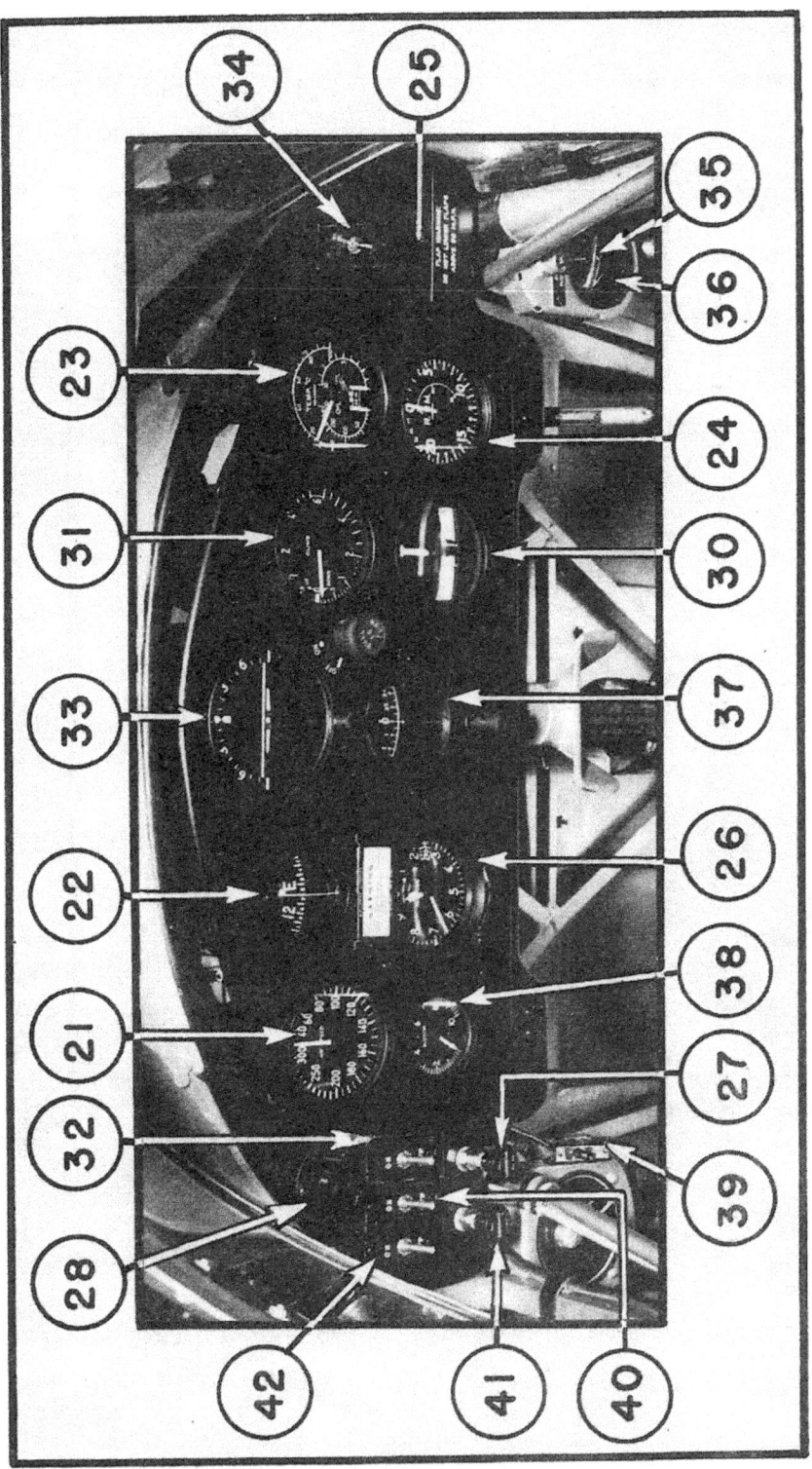

Figure 16 - PT-26 Instrument Panel

21. AIR SPEED INDICATOR
22. COMPASS
    PT-19, PT-19A - FRONT COCKPITS ONLY
    PT-19B, PT-23 - REAR COCKPIT ONLY
    PT-26 - BOTH COCKPITS
23. ENGINE GAGE UNIT
24. TACHOMETER
25. CLOCK
    PT-19, PT-19A - FRONT COCKPITS ONLY
    PT-19B, PT-23 - BOTH COCKPITS
    PT-26 - REAR COCKPIT ONLY
26. ALTIMETER
27. CARBURETOR AIR HEAT CONTROL
28. INSTRUMENT LIGHT SWITCH AND RHEOSTAT
30. TURN AND BANK INDICATOR
31. RATE OF CLIMB INDICATOR
32. VOLTAGE BOOSTER (INVERTER) SWITCH
33. GYRO HORIZON
34. LANDING LIGHT SWITCH
35. GENERATOR BRAKE CONTROL
    PT-26 - FRONT COCKPIT ONLY
36. AMMETER
    PT-26 - FRONT COCKPIT ONLY
37. DIRECTIONAL GYRO
38. SUCTION GAGE
39. OIL DILUTION SWITCH
40. TAILLIGHT SWITCH
41. COCKPIT HEATER CONTROL
42. WING LIGHTS SWITCH

- 7 -

RESTRICTED

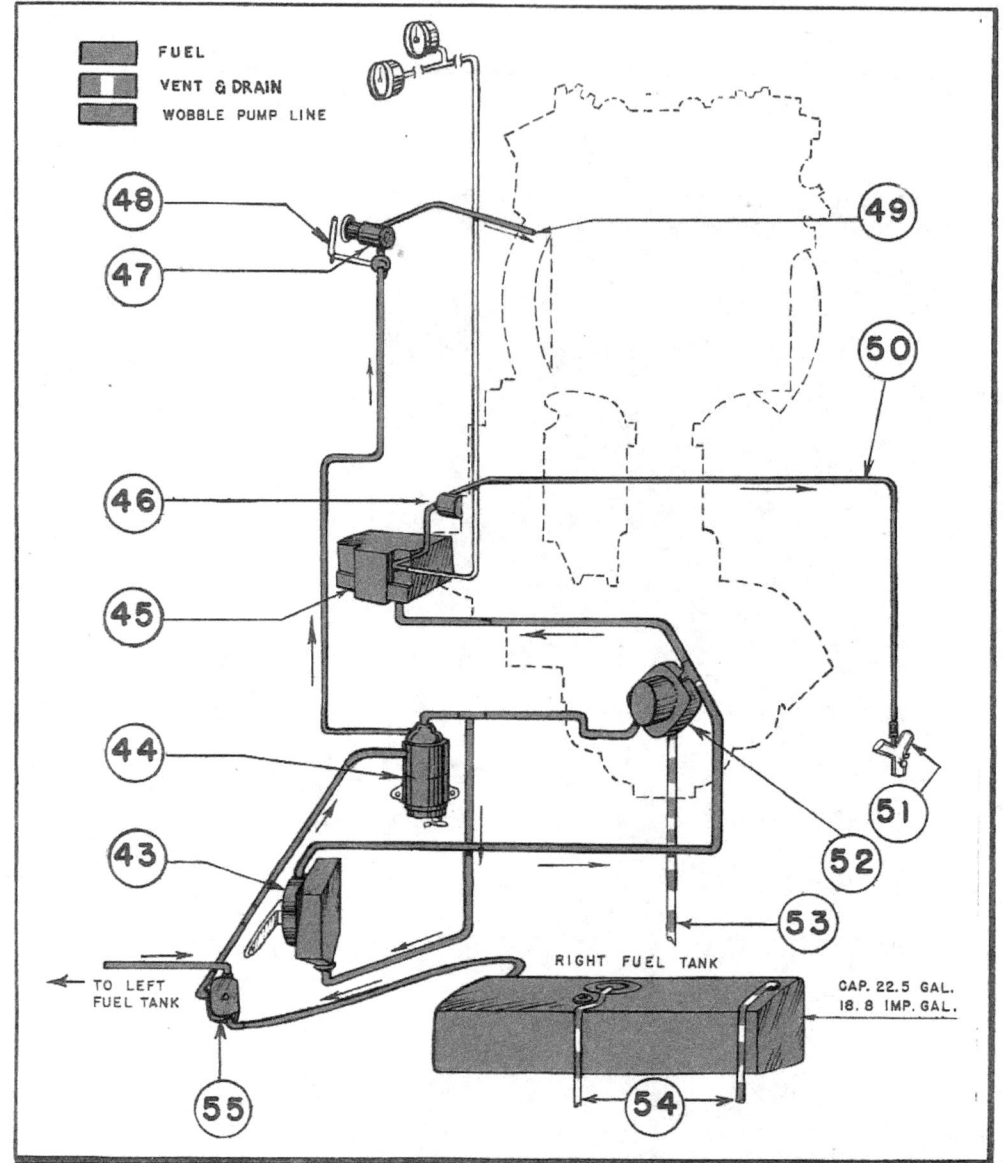

Figure 17 - Fuel System - PT-19, PT-19A, PT-19B, PT-26

43. WOBBLE PUMP
44. FUEL STRAINER
45. CARBURETOR
46. SOLENOID (PT-19B, PT-23, PT-26 ONLY)
47. PRIMER
48. PRIMER SHUT-OFF
49. PRIMER LINE TO MANIFOLD
50. OIL DILUTION LINE (PT-19B, PT-23, PT-26 ONLY)
51. Y-DRAIN VALVE
52. FUEL PUMP
53. DRAIN LINE FROM PUMP
54. TANK VENT LINES
55. FUEL SELECTOR VALVE

RESTRICTED   T. O. No. 01-115GA-1

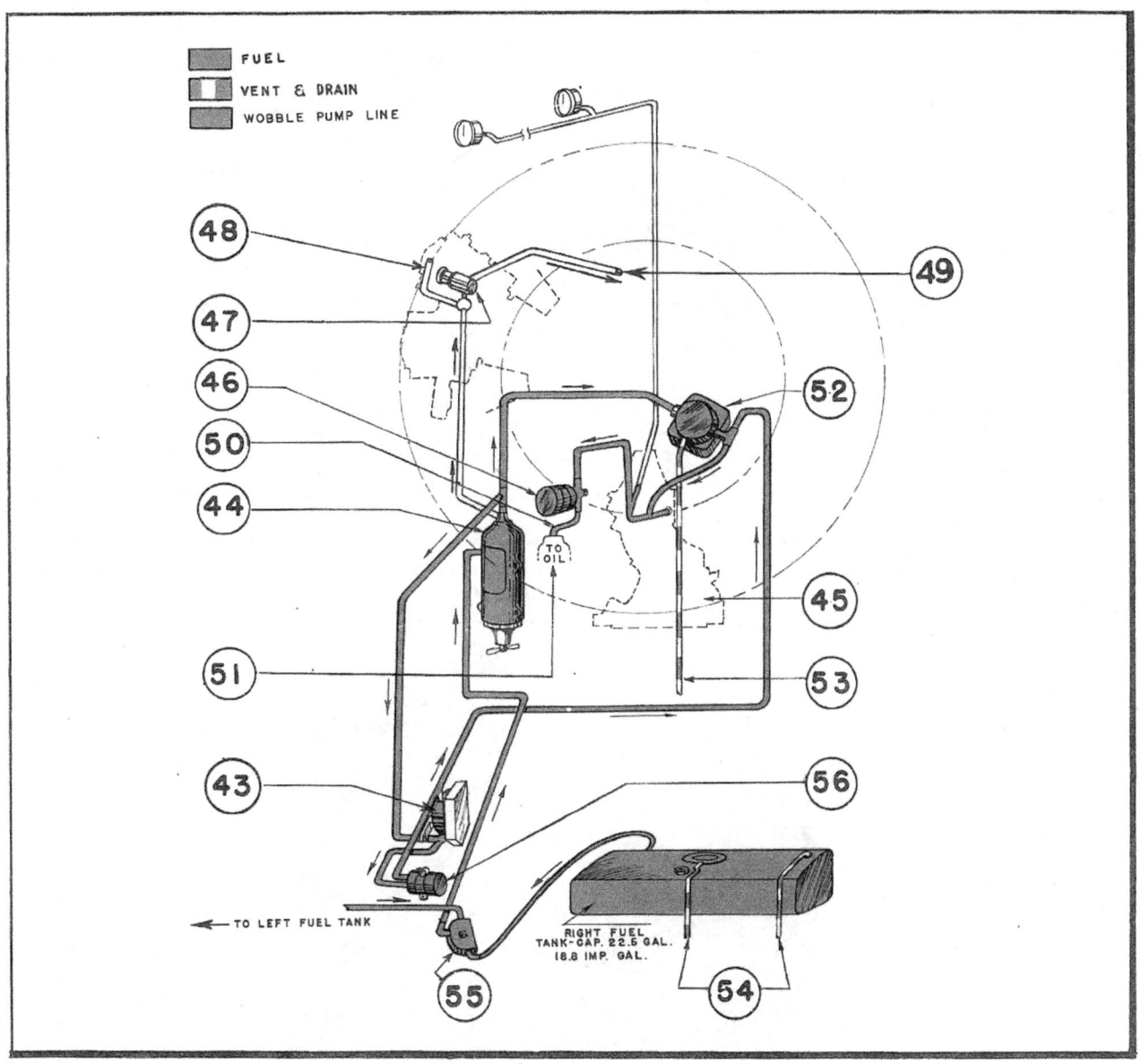

Figure 18 - Fuel System - PT-23

43. WOBBLE PUMP

44. FUEL STRAINER

45. CARBURETOR

46. SOLENOID (PT-19B, PT-23, PT-26 ONLY)

47. PRIMER

48. PRIMER SHUT-OFF

49. PRIMER LINE TO MANIFOLD

50. OIL DILUTION LINE (PT-19B, PT-23, PT-26 ONLY)

51. Y-DRAIN VALVE

52. FUEL PUMP

53. DRAIN LINE FROM PUMP

54. TANK VENT LINES

55. FUEL SELECTOR VALVE

56. RELIEF VALVE (TYPE A-1) USED ONLY WITH F-10 FUEL PUMP. NOT USED WITH G-6 FUEL PUMP

RESTRICTED   T. O. No. 01-115GA-1

57. OIL TEMPERATURE
    REGULATOR (COOLER)

58. TANK VENT LINE

59. LINE TO OIL
    SEPARATOR

60. OIL "IN" LINE AND
    TANK DRAIN

61. OIL DILUTION LINE
    TO SOLENOID

62. OIL TEMPERATURE
    LINES

63. DRAIN VALVE

64. OIL "IN" LINE AND
    ENGINE DRAIN

65. SCUPPER DRAIN LINE

66. OIL RETURN LINE,
    COOLER TO TANK

67. OIL RETURN LINE,
    ENGINE TO COOLER
    ENGINE BREATHER LINE
    AND PRESSURE LINES
    NOT SHOWN.

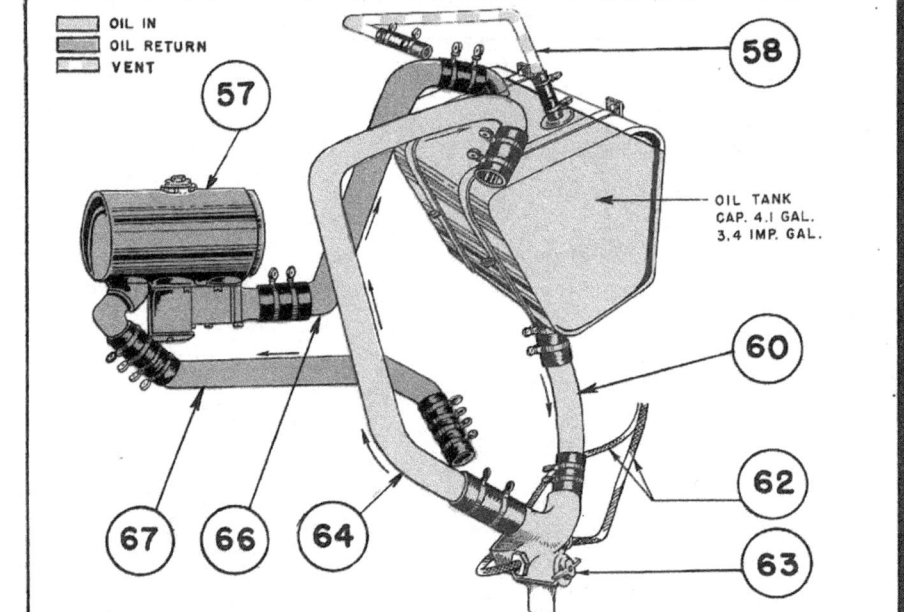

Figure 19 - Oil System - PT-19, PT-19A
Figure 20 - Oil System - PT-19B, PT-26

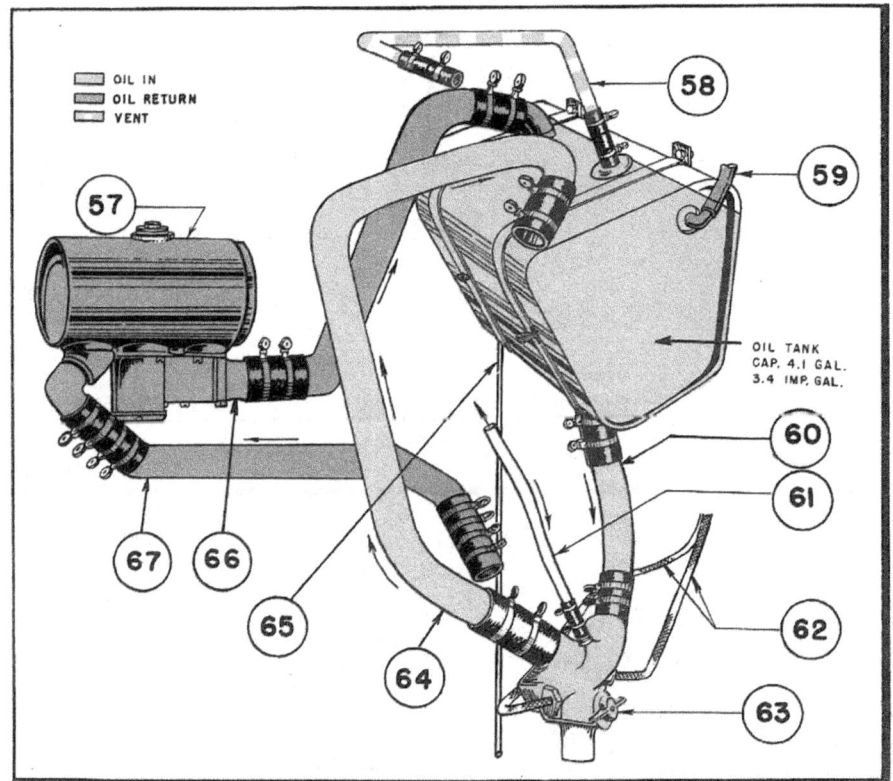

- 10 -   RESTRICTED

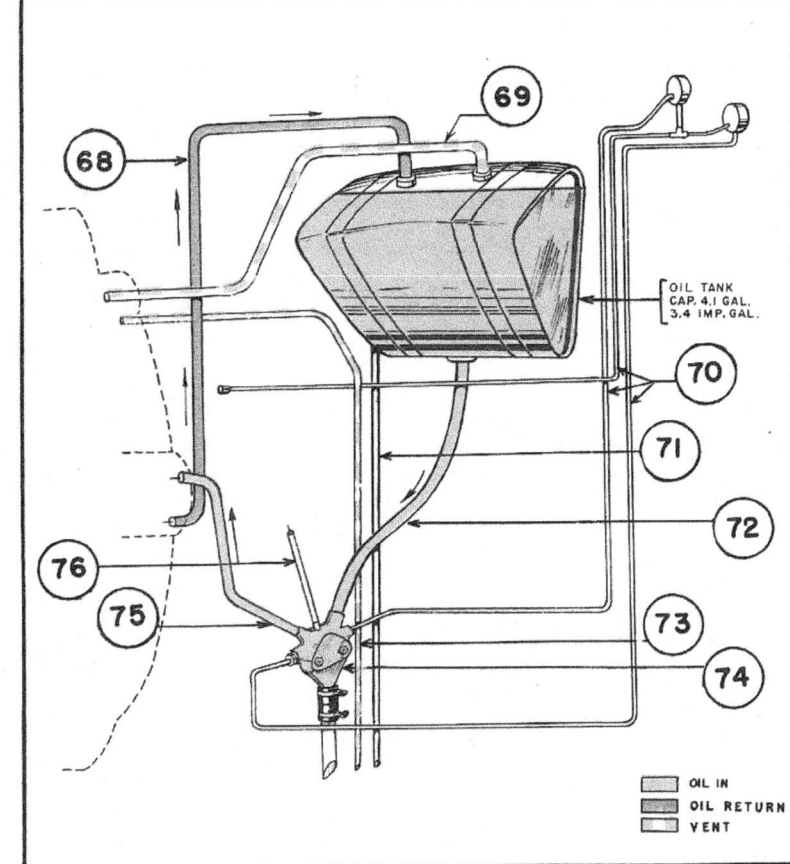

68. OIL RETURN LINE
69. VENT LINE, ENGINE TO TANK
70. OIL TEMPERATURE AND PRESSURE LINES
71. SCUPPER DRAIN LINE
72. OIL "IN" LINE AND TANK DRAIN
73. ENGINE BREATHER LINE
74. DRAIN VALVE
75. OIL "IN" LINE AND ENGINE DRAIN
76. OIL DILUTION LINE TO SOLENOID

Figure 21 - Oil System PT-23

b. FUEL SYSTEM. - The center wing section is fitted with two fuel tanks, one on each side of the fuselage. Capacity of each tank is 22.5 gallons (18.7 Imperial gallons). There is no reserve or auxiliary tank. Each tank is filled by first removing the cover plate, held in place by a Dzus fastener, in the top surface of the center section. The filler cap is directly beneath the cover plate. PT-26 ONLY has a grounding jack, outboard from each tank cover plate, into which the fuel grounding wire should be plugged while filling tanks. A direct reading magnetic fuel gage, visible from both cockpits, is fitted into the top of each tank and projects through the top surface of the center section. The gage is correct only when in flying position. A conventional fuel selector valve is located on the left side of each cockpit below the instrument panel. When turning valve, be careful to feel that it is seated in the new position. In building up fuel pressure prior to starting the engine, three or four strokes of the wobble pump handle are used. This handle is mounted on the left side of each cockpit by the seat. A pressure of 2.5 to 3.5 pounds is desired to start the engine which is then maintained by the engine-driven fuel pump. The hand-operated wobble pump is used in the event the engine-driven pump fails in flight.

c. OIL SYSTEM. - The oil tank is secured to the engine mount, and filler cap is accessible through a door in the engine cowl. Tank capacity is 4.1 gallons (3.4 Imperial gallons).

(1) PT-19, PT-19A, PT-19B, PT-26 ONLY. - Maximum permissible pressure is 70 pounds per square inch. Minimum 50 pounds per square inch. Desired pressure is 60 pounds per square inch.

(2) PT-23 ONLY. - Maximum permissible pressure is 90 pounds per square inch. Minimum 60 pounds per square inch. Desired pressure is 75 pounds per square inch.

(3) OIL DILUTION - PT-26 ONLY. - For cold weather starting or emergency operation, a switch below the left side of instrument panel is provided to allow fuel to flow into the oil lines and dilute the oil. This switch should never by left "ON" over 15 seconds at any one time and should be used prior to stopping the engine at the end of an operation period so as to facilitate the next starting.

d. ELECTRICAL SYSTEM - PT-19B, PT-23 ONLY. Electric power is supplied by a 24-volt engine-driven generator through a 24-volt storage battery mounted on the rear structure of the front seat. The master switch is on the right side of the front cockpit and may be operated only in the front cockpit. Master switch must be turned "ON" before operation of any electrical equipment.

(1) NAVIGATION LIGHTS. - Switch for navigation lights is on left side of each instrument panel. "DOWN" position of switch is momentary and turns navigation light "ON" for signaling purposes only. Use "UP" position of switch for constant operation of lights.

(2) INSTRUMENT LIGHTS. - Rheostat to adjust amount of light desired is on left side of each panel. Each light is manually operated on a ball socket fitting on the left side of each cockpit.

(3) INTERPHONE. - A type RC-73-A electrical interphone system permits conversation from front to rear cockpit only. The microphone is of conventional "press-to-talk" type.

(4) PT-26 ONLY. - Electrical system is similar to that in the PT-19B and PT-23 but is 12 volts instead of 24 volts, and electrical interphone is not installed. The generator is wind-driven, mounted on the lower side of the center section. A generator brake control below the right side of the front instrument panel is used to stop the generator when desired. The engine-driven generator is not used. An ammeter adjacent to the generator brake control indicates the charging rate. A voltage "booster" or inverter, operated by a switch on the left side of each panel, is used in the instrument light system to step the voltage up to 24. One switch is provided for wing navigation lights and another for tail navigation light, both on left side of each panel. PT-26 has a landing light in the right wing operated by a switch on the right side of each panel. Master switch may be turned "ON" in the front or rear cockpit.

(5) PT-19 AND PT-19A. - No electrical equipment.

e. ENGINE CONTROLS.

(1) THROTTLE CONTROL. - Conventional.

(2) MIXTURE CONTROL. - Full forward for full-rich mixture on all models except PT-26. On PT-26 full aft for full-rich mixture and forward for lean mixture.

(a) "FULL RICH" is the setting of the mixture control lever in the position giving maximum fuel flow.

(b) "BEST POWER" (sometimes termed "MAXIMUM POWER") is the setting of the control lever which, with a given fixed throttle setting, results in the maximum engine rpm at the leanest fuel flow; that is, further leaning of the mixture would cause a decrease in engine rpm.

(c) "RICH BEST POWER" is the setting of the mixture control lever which, with a given fixed throttle setting, results in the maximum engine rpm at the richest fuel flow.

(d) "SMOOTH OPERATION." - To obtain the setting for "SMOOTH OPERATION," the setting for "BEST POWER" is obtained and the mixture enriched until engine speed drops from 20 to 30 rpm.

(e) "MAXIMUM ECONOMY" is obtained by adjusting to "BEST POWER" and then leaning to obtain a decrease of 40 to 50 rpm.

(3) IGNITION SWITCHES. - A conventional ignition switch is installed in the left side of the front cockpit which may also be controlled from the rear cockpit through an extension, mounted through a dummy switch.

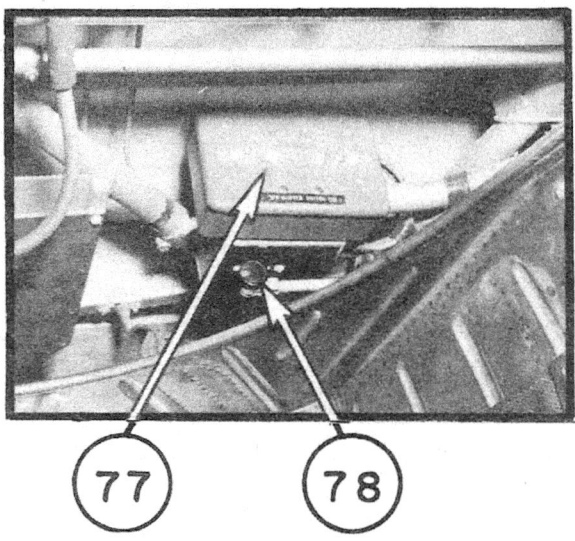

Figure 22 - Fuse Box and Master Switch - PT-26
77. FUSE BOX   78. MASTER SWITCH

Figure 23 - Throttle and Mixture Controls - PT-19, PT-19A PT-19B, PT-23

(4) CARBURETOR HEATER CONTROL. - Located on left side of each instrument panel. Pull full out to "ON" position at the slightest indication of carburetor icing.

f. HEATING AND VENTILATING EQUIPMENT - PT-26 ONLY. - Main heater valve is operated by a control on the left side of either cockpit. Individual shutters in the floor of each cockpit, operated by the occupant, control the amount of heat released to each

RESTRICTED T. O. No. 01-115GA-1

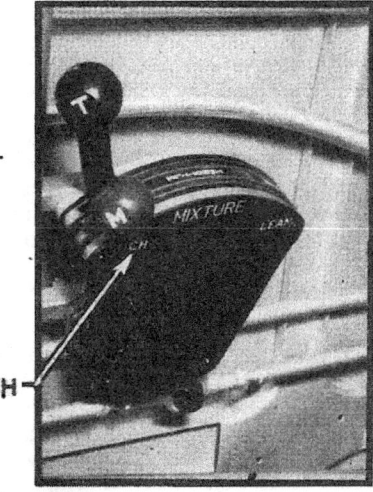

Figure 24 - Throttle and Mixture Controls - PT-26

eration of the turn and bank indicators, gyro horizons, and directional gyros. This system eliminates the use of venturi tubes and requires no operation by the pilot. On PT-26 ONLY a suction gage connected with the system is on the left side of each instrument panel. Three and one-half to 4 inches of mercury should be indicated for proper operation of the system.

(b) PT-23 ONLY. - Vacuum is obtained by the use of two type A-3 venturi tubes and no engine-driven vacuum system is installed.

(2) SPEAKING TUBE - PT-19, PT-19A, PT-26 ONLY. - A nonelectric speaking tube is provided for communication from front to rear cockpit. Other models have electric interphone system as described in paragraph (4) under "Electrical System."

(3) BAGGAGE COMPARTMENT. - Starter crank is stowed in baggage compartment when not in use. It is held in place by clips fastened to baggage compartment door or floor.

(a) PT-19, PT-19A, PT-19B, PT-23 ONLY. - A 3-cubic foot baggage compartment is located inside rear deck and is accessible through door in left side of rear deck.

Figure 25 - Controls, Left Side

Figure 26 - Cockpit Heater Shutter - PT-26

cockpit. For normal ventilation the cockpit enclosure may be opened to the first position in either or both cockpits.

g. MISCELLANEOUS FUSELAGE EQUIPMENT.

(1) INSTRUMENTS AND CONTROLS.

(a) VACUUM SYSTEM - PT-19B, PT-26 ONLY. An engine-driven vacuum pump supplies a vacuum through an oil separator and relief valve for the op-

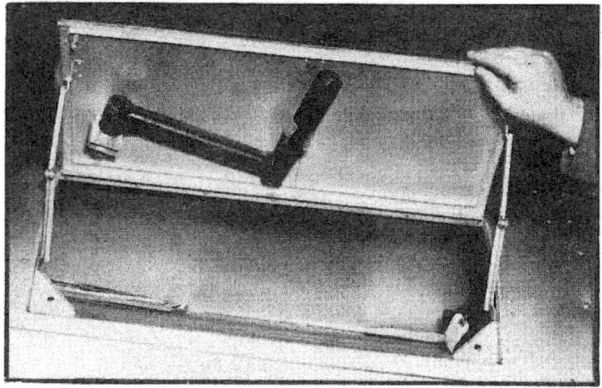

Figure 27 - Baggage Compartment - PT-19, PT-19A, PT-19B, PT-23

- 13 -

RESTRICTED

(b) PT-26 ONLY. - Baggage compartment is accessible through door behind rear seat.

(4) REARVIEW MIRROR. - A round adjustable rearview mirror is located on the top right portion of the front windshield.

(5) FLIGHT REPORT HOLDER. - A type A-2 flight report holder is provided in the front cockpit.

(6) DATA CASE. - A data case is provided in the rear cockpit.

(7) SAFETY BELTS.

(a) PT-19 and PT-19A ONLY through AAF serial No. 42-34061 are equipped with standard safety belts. PT-19A after AAF serial No. 42-34062 incorporates two Sutton-type shoulder harnesses.

(b) PT-19B, PT-23, and PT-26 are equipped with Sutton-type shoulder harnesses.

(8) BLIND FLYING HOOD - PT-19B, PT-23, PT-26 ONLY. - For instrument flying instructions, a hood is provided in the rear cockpit. It is pulled forward by the occupant over his head. When not in use it is held back of the seat by shock cord tension on both sides of the cockpit.

4. FLYING CHARACTERISTICS.

a. GENERAL. - All models are exceptionally stable over a wide speed range and under all normal locations of the center of gravity. Lateral control is good down to the stall point. Controls are all of ball-bearing type, hence very responsive and light. General flight characteristics are good. PT-23 ONLY of the five models, the PT-23 is comparatively light at the tail, but this condition does not make the flight or ground characteristics appreciably different from the other models.

b. TAXYING. - The steerable and automatic swivel tail wheel contributes to the ease of taxying. Brakes have no tendency to grab, and the airplane is easy to handle even in severe cross-winds. Do not use brakes any more than necessary in taxying.

c. TAKE-OFF. - Take-off speed for all models is about 60 mph. This speed gives a clean take-off without any tendency to bounce or struggle into the air. The use of flaps for take-off is not recommended. During take-off, right rudder pressure is necessary to counteract for torque until flying speed is attained.

d. CLIMBING. - Elevator tab should be adjusted to properly trim the airplane immediately after leaving the ground. This adjustment usually is to the "O" mark on the elevator tab indicators. Full throttle should be used for all climbs to assure proper engine cooling. Best climbing speed for all models is 80 mph.

e. NORMAL FLIGHT. - Elevator tab should be adjusted for level flight depending upon the individual loading condition. Correct engine rpm for cruising:

(1) PT-19, PT-19A, PT-19B - 2065 rpm.

(2) PT-23 - 1800 rpm.

(3) PT-26 - 2065 rpm.

f. STALLS. - A complete stall is followed by an abrupt drop of the nose with no tendency for the airplane to fall off on either wing. ON PT-23 nose must be brought up higher than on other models for full stall. Right rudder is used in all power stalls to compensate for torque. Stalling speeds are:

(1) PT-19, PT-19A - 58 mph.

(2) PT-19B, PT-23, PT-26 - 61 mph.

Recovering from stalls should not be attempted at less than 80 mph.

g. SPINS. - The spinning characteristics of all models are good, and recovery should be made with full opposite rudder, followed immediately by momentarily applying forward stick pressure.

h. DIVING. - Diving above 191 mph is prohibited.

i. AEROBATICS. - All models are adequately stressed for all regularly taught aerobatics. Inverted flight for protracted periods of time will result in cutting off the fuel and oil supply to the engine.

j. MANEUVERS PROHIBITED. - Outside loops and any maneuvers producing negative loads must not be attempted.

k. APPROACH FOR LANDING. - Trim the airplane to glide in at 80 mph. NEVER LOWER FLAPS OVER 95 MPH. The use of half flaps is recommended in primary training stages and full flaps for later stages of training.

l. LANDING. - Landing characteristics are conventional. The wide landing gear, low center of gravity location and steerable tail wheel contribute to the absence of any tendency to ground loop. In making cross-wind landings, a normal approach is made and drift removed immediately before touching the ground.

SECTION III

FLIGHT AND GENERAL OPERATING INSTRUCTIONS

1. ON ENTERING THE COCKPIT.

   a. SPECIAL CHECK FOR NIGHT FLYING - PT-19B AND PT-26 ONLY.

   (1) Master switch "ON."

   (2) Voltage booster switch "ON" (PT-26 ONLY).

   (3) Instrument light rheostat "ON."

   (4) Test operate navigation lights; one switch on PT-19B, two on PT-26.

   (5) Test operate landing light (PT-26 ONLY).

   b. CHECK FOR ALL FLIGHTS.

   (1) Ignition switch "OFF."

   (2) Flaps "UP."

   (3) Disengage control lock and check freedom of movement of flight controls.

   (4) Parking brake "ON."

   (5) Fuel selector valve on "RIGHT" or "LEFT" tank.

   (6) Throttle "CLOSED."

   (7) Mixture "FULL RICH."

   (8) Carburetor air heat "OFF" (in).

2. PROCEDURE PRELIMINARY TO STARTING.

   a. If the engine has been idle for over 30 minutes or if excessive priming has been used during starting attempts, make certain that ignition is turned to the "OFF" position, open the throttle wide, and crank the engine by hand four or five revolutions. If fuel or oil is present in any combustion chamber as evidenced by excessive compression, remove the spark plugs from the cylinder, drain all liquid from the cylinder and intake pipes and dry spark plugs thoroughly before replacing.

   CAUTION Starting the engine with excessive oil or fuel in the cylinders will result in bent or broken rods.

   b. In cold weather, it may be necessary to preheat the oil before starting if the oil dilution system has not been used.

   c. Set the mixture control to the "FULL RICH" position.

   d. Operate the wobble pump to obtain a fuel pressure of 2-1/2 to 3-1/2 pounds per square inch. (PT-23, 2 to 3 pounds.)

   e. Move throttle lever almost to "CLOSED" position, or about one-eighth open.

   f. Master switch "ON" (PT-19B, PT-23 and PT-26 ONLY).

3. STARTING.

   a. Prime engine (if necessary) with two or three strokes of the prime pump. Avoid overpriming. If overprimed, proceed as outlined in paragraph 2.a. In cold weather, two or three strokes of the primer and four sharp strokes of the throttle should be applied. On PT-23, use six to eight shots of primer only. Do not pump throttle on PT-23.

   b. Turn ignition switch "ON" to "LEFT" position (PT-19, PT-19A, PT-19B, and PT-26). On PT-23 ignition switch should be placed on "BOTH."

   NOTE USE ONLY LEFT-HAND MAGNETO ON PT-19, PT-19A, PT-19B, and PT-26 FOR STARTING. THIS MAGNETO IS EQUIPPED WITH AN IMPULSE COUPLING WHICH PROVIDES THE STARTING BOOST.

   c. Start engine with direct cranking hand starter on PT-19, PT-19A, PT-19B, and PT-26. On PT-23, hand inertia starter is used.

   d. Immediately on starting of the engine, close throttle and turn ignition switch to "BOTH" (PT-19, PT-19A, PT-19B and PT-26). Under extremely cold conditions, a rapid pumping of the throttle near the "CLOSED" position may be required for the first minute after the engine starts. Do not pump throttle on PT-23.

   WARNING STOP ENGINE IF OIL PRESSURE DOES NOT REGISTER WITHIN 30 SECONDS AFTER STARTING.

   e. When the engine starts firing evenly, return primer to "LOCKED" position and slowly open the throttle to 600 to 800 rpm for warm-up.

4. WARM-UP AND GROUND TEST.

   a. GENERAL. - The following paragraphs prescribe ground tests which will be performed prior to flight.

   (1) The engine will be stopped rather than idled for prolonged periods after warm-up has been ac-

complished. It is desirable to nose the airplane into the wind during warm-up.

(2) Any faulty operation or malfunctioning noted during these ground tests will be investigated and the necessary adjustment made prior to take-off.

(3) After engine is thoroughly warm, testing should be accomplished as quickly as possible. Avoid prolonged running on the ground.

(4) All ground testing and running of engine will be accomplished with carburetor mixture control set at "FULL RICH" (PT-19, PT-19A, PT-19B and PT-26). On PT-23, all ground testing and running of engine will be accomplished with carburetor set at "SMOOTH OPERATION" position.

b. OIL PRESSURE AND TEMPERATURE CHECK.

(1) Engine will always be warmed up on the ground until proper lubrication and engine operation for take-off and flight are assured.

(2) As soon as the engine has started, watch the oil gage for pressure. If the oil pressure gage does not indicate 50 pounds per square inch pressure within 1/2 minute, shut down the engine and make an investigation.

(3) The warming-up period is important and should be carried out as follows:

(a) After the oil gage indicates pressure, run the engine at 800 to 1000 rpm until the pressure is normal for this speed, which will be a value between 50 to 70 pounds per square inch. Run PT-23 between 700 and 800 rpm. (Desired normal oil pressure PT-23 only, 60 to 80 pounds.)

(b) The warming-up period should be extended for at least 5 minutes after which the speed can be increased to 1000 to 1200 rpm. These speeds should not be exceeded until the oil-in temperature registers 35°C (95°F).

(c) Fuel pressure should be 2-1/2 to 3-1/2 pounds on PT-19, PT-19A, PT-19B and PT-26; 2 to 3 pounds on PT-23.

c. IGNITION SYSTEM CHECK.

(1) After engine is thoroughly warm, open throttle to obtain 1900 rpm for ignition check.

(2) Note the loss of rpm when switched to one magneto at a time. It is important to switch back to "BOTH" and leave switch in that position until the engine has picked up the loss in rpm resulting from operating on one magneto before testing for loss in rpm on the other magneto. The normal loss in rpm when operating on one magneto should not exceed 100 rpm. This check should be made by running on each magneto for approximately 5 seconds. On PT-23 ONLY, maximum drop should be 75 rpm at 1600 rpm.

(3) To assure the proper connection of the magneto ground wire, the "OFF" position of the ignition switch should be checked at the end of the warm-up period. With the engine turning over at about 700 rpm, turn ignition switch momentarily to "OFF" position, and immediately return to the "BOTH ON" position. If engine does not entirely cease firing when switch is in "OFF" position, inspect ground at magneto and crankcase.

WARNING IF ENGINE DOES NOT CEASE FIRING WHEN THE SWITCH IS IN THE "OFF" POSITION, IT WILL BE NECESSARY TO STOP THE ENGINE BY SHIFTING THE MIXTURE CONTROL TO THE "IDLE CUT-OFF" POSITION.

(4) After warm-up has been completed, minimum wide-open ground rpm should be 1900 on PT-19, PT-19A, PT-19B and PT-26. Minimum wide-open ground rpm should be 1810 on PT-23 ONLY.

5. TAXIING.

a. Flaps "UP."

b. Keep clear of tall grass, mud holes, and loose stones. Turn airplane as necessary to maintain good forward visibility; taxi slowly.

6. TAKE-OFF.

a. PREFLIGHT CHECK.

(1) TAB CONTROL. - Adjust as follows, using indicator DIVISIONS as guide, starting from neutral position (determine visually). Indicator NUMERALS are not reliable for initial setting.

PT-19, PT-19A, PT-19B, and PT-26

Both seats occupied, 3 DIVISIONS nose-up direction. Rear seat only occupied, 2 DIVISIONS nose-up direction. Front seat only occupied, 7 DIVISIONS nose-up direction.

PT-23

Both seats occupied, 6 DIVISIONS nose-up direction. Rear seat only occupied, 5 DIVISIONS nose-up direction. Front seat only occupied, 8 DIVISIONS nose-up direction.

(2) Carburetor air heat "OFF" (in), unless icing conditions are present.

(3) Flaps "UP."

(4) Fuel selector valve on RIGHT or LEFT tank.

(5) Check flight controls for free operation.

(6) Release parking brake.

b. Do not start take-off with the cylinder head temperature above 205°C (401°F).

c. Check to see that mixture control is in the

"FULL RICH" position. It should remain in this position during take-off and climb.

d. Throttle wide open.

e. Readjust tab control as necessary as soon as airplane is in the air.

7. ENGINE FAILURE DURING TAKE-OFF.

a. Ignition switch "OFF."

b. Drop nose and maintain a gliding speed of about 80 mph STRAIGHT AHEAD. DO NOT ATTEMPT TO TURN BACK INTO THE FIELD.

c. Open cockpit enclosure (PT-26 ONLY).

8. CLIMBING.

a. All climbs are made with full throttle to assure proper engine cooling.

b. Mixture control "FULL RICH" to 5000 feet.

c. Best climbing speed is 80 mph.

9. FLIGHT.

a. The rpm, oil temperature, and oil pressure give the most satisfactory indication of the engine's performance. If any one of these appear irregular, the engine should be throttled down, and if the cause cannot be eliminated, a landing should be made to investigate and correct the difficulty.

b. For flying characteristics, refer to paragraph 4., section II, and applicable engine flight charts.

c. Cruising, 2065 rpm and maximum cruising 2230 rpm for PT-19, PT-19A, PT-19B and PT-26. Cruising 1800 rpm and maximum cruising 1890 rpm for PT-23 ONLY.

d. Maximum allowable rpm 2600 for PT-19, PT-19A, PT-19B and PT-26; 2490 rpm for PT-23.

e. Maximum allowable speed 191 mph.

f. Oil pressure should be 50 pounds minimum and 70 pounds maximum for PT-19, PT-19A, PT-19B and PT-26; for PT-23 only, 60 pounds minimum, 90 pounds maximum.

g. Oil temperature should be 60°C (140°F) to 77°C (170°F) normal; 93°C (199°F) maximum. PT-23 ONLY, 95°C (203°F) maximum.

h. Fuel pressure should be 2-1/2 to 3-1/2 pounds on PT-19, PT-19A, PT-19B and PT-26; 2 to 3 pounds on PT-23 ONLY.

i. Suction (vacuum system) should be 3-1/2 to 4 inches of mercury (PT-26 ONLY).

j. Mixture should be "FULL RICH" under 5,000 feet. Adjust for smooth operation above 5,000 feet.

k. Carburetor air heat "OFF" (in) unless required by icing conditions.

10. ENGINE FAILURE DURING FLIGHT.

a. Follow applicable instructions in paragraphs 11. and 12. following.

b. Ignition switch "OFF" in glide.

c. Master switch "OFF" after landing.

11. APPROACH FOR LANDING.

a. Fuel selector valve turned to tank containing most fuel.

b. Mixture "FULL RICH."

c. Carburetor air heat "OFF" (in) unless required by icing conditions.

d. Flaps "DOWN." Use of half flaps is recommended in initial training stages, full flaps for advanced stages. DO NOT LOWER FLAPS ABOVE 95 MPH.

e. Gliding speed, 80 mph.

f. Adjust tab control as required.

g. Open cockpit enclosure (PT-26 ONLY).

12. LANDING.

a. From cruising condition, slowly close throttle to idling rpm and check to see that the mixture control is set at "FULL RICH."

NOTE When landing in fields of above 5000 feet altitude, the mixture control should be maintained in the position which has been found to give "SMOOTH OPERATION" as defined in section II, paragraph 3.e.

b. Care should be exercised to prevent overcooling of the engine during long glides.

c. Periodic low rpm "bursts" of the engine will insure clean spark plugs and a warm engine ready for instantaneous emergency application of power.

d. Land the airplane gently. Do not attempt to get down too rapidly and do not level off too high.

e. CROSS-WIND LANDING. - Proceed as in normal landing and remove all drift just before touching the ground.

f. Flaps "UP" after rolling to a stop.

13. EMERGENCY TAKE-OFF IF LANDING IS NOT COMPLETED.

a. Throttle "WIDE OPEN."

b. Flaps "UP" gradually, after reaching 80 mph and 200 feet altitude.

14. STOPPING ENGINE.

a. Apply toe brakes and engage parking brake.

b. The engine should be stopped as soon as possible in the following manner:

(1) Leaving the fuel valve "ON" open the throttle slowly until the engine speed is from 800 to 1000 rpm. Shift the mixture control to the "FULL LEAN" or "IDLE CUT-OFF" position and continue moving the throttle slowly to the wide open position. This causes the engine to cut out if the engine speed has been kept under 1000 rpm. The cut-out is especially abrupt in carburetors equipped with an idle cut-off.

(2) Turn the ignition switch to the "OFF" position after the engine ceases firing.

(3) Leave the mixture control in the "FULL LEAN" of "IDLE CUT-OFF" position as a precaution against accidental starting.

c. When air temperature is 40°F or below, use oil dilution switch before stopping engine if airplane is not to be used again within 30 minutes to 1 hour (PT-26 ONLY).

(1) Operate engine at 1000 to 1200 rpm.

(2) Maintain oil temperature well below 50°C (122°F) and oil pressure above 15 pounds per square inch. (If necessary, stop engine and after oil has cooled to below 40°C, restart engine and proceed with oil dilution.)

(3) Dilute engine oil by turning "ON" switch marked "OIL DILUTION" for approximately the time limits as follows, for ground temperatures shown.

4°	to	-12°C	(40° to 10°F)	2 minutes
-12°	to	-29°C	(10° to -20°F)	4 minutes
-29°	to	-46°C	(-20° to -50°F)	See note

NOTE A dilution period exceeding 4 minutes to provide the required dilution is excessive for this aircraft, and for operation at ground temperature below -29°C (-20°F), external heat in addition to the maximum dilution is necessary. More dilution can be obtained by increasing the time period, but excessive amounts of fuel are being added to the oil system, oil temperatures rise above 50°C, and the oil capacity is reduced.

(4) The dilution of the engine oil while the oil temperatures are above 50°C is not particularly effective. In some instances, particularly during sub-zero temperature, where a long dilution period is required, the engine oil temperature may rise above the maximum desired values for oil dilution (50°C). If this occurs, it may be necessary to dilute the oil in two or more short periods. If it is necessary to service the oil tank, the dilution procedure must be divided so that some dilution is accomplished before servicing the oil tank, and the remainder is accomplished after the oil tank is serviced. After dilution has been accomplished, shut off the engine in the normal manner, continuing to hold the dilution valve on until the engine stops.

(5) When 50 hours engine time has elapsed since the last oil dilution was accomplished, two or more dilutions will be used instead of one. On these occasions, the engine will be given the full dilution period and after each dilution, the engine will be shut down and the oil pressure screens will be removed and cleaned. This is necessary because the fuel in the oil tends to wash down any accumulated sludge within the engine. After reinstallation of the oil screens, the engine will be started and run for at least 20 minutes at 1000 to 1200 rpm to evaporate any fuel in the oil. The engine will then again be diluted for the usual period of time.

(6) In starting the engine, a normal start should be made without regard to the oil dilution system.

NOTE It is necessary to operate an aircraft engine at normal operating temperatures for approximately 1/2 hour to permit the fuel in the oil supply to evaporate and cause the oil to resume its normal viscosity. High temperatures will shorten this time period slightly.

(7) Engines which suddenly show a loss in oil pressure or throw oil out the breathers during flight, will be checked upon landing to insure that the oil dilution valve is in the "CLOSED" position and fully seated.

15. BEFORE LEAVING THE COCKPIT.

a. Fuel selector valve "OFF."

b. All light switches "OFF." (PT-19B, PT-23, and PT-26.)

c. Master switch "OFF." (PT-19B, PT-23, and PT-26.)

d. Engage control lock.

16. MANEUVERS PROHIBITED.

a. Outside loops.

b. Any maneuvers which might impose negative loads on any part of the airplane.

c. Snap rolls in excess of 100 mph.

d. Immelman turns in excess of 170 mph.

e. Slow rolls in excess of 150 mph.

f. Indicated airspeed in excess of 191 mph.

SECTION IV

FLIGHT OPERATION DATA

1. DETERMINING GROSS WEIGHT.

   a. Refer to the "WEIGHT AND BALANCE CHART" in this section for the applicable model airplane, and check the listed basic and alternate tabulated items against those loaded in the airplane. If the airplane is loaded in accordance with the "Basic Load Items" whose weights are entered in the "Pounds" column, and, the "Alternate Items" whose weights are entered under two loading conditions in the "Alternate Loading (Pounds)" column, the gross weight will be found listed at the bottom of the chart. If any items tabulated in the "Pounds" columns are omitted in the loading of the airplane, deduct the weight of the missing items from the "Gross Weight," and the answer will be correct gross weight as the airplane is actually loaded.

   b. Baggage, not to exceed the allowable weight listed under "Alternate Items," may be carried when secured with tie-down straps in the baggage compartment.

2. FLIGHT PLANNING.

   The following outline may be used as a guide to assist personnel in the use of the FLIGHT OPERATION INSTRUCTION CHART for flight planning purposes.

   a. If the flight plan calls for a continuous flight where the desired cruising power and air speed are reasonably constant after take-off and climb to 5000 feet, the fuel required and flight time may be computed as a "single section flight."

   (1) Within the limits of the airplane, the fuel required and flying time for a given mission depend largely upon the speed desired. With all other factors remaining equal in an airplane, speed is obtained at a sacrifice of range, and range is obtained at a sacrifice of speed. The speed is usually determined after considering the urgency of the flight plotted against the range required. The time of take-off is adjusted so as to have the flight arrive at its destination at the predetermined time.

   (2) Select the FLIGHT OPERATION INSTRUCTION CHART for the model airplane and gross weight to be used at take-off. Locate the largest figure entered under G.P.H. (gallons per hour) in column 1 on the lower half of the chart. Multiply this figure by the number and/or fraction of hours desired for reserve fuel. Add the resulting figure to the number of gallons set forth in footnote No. 2, and subtract the total from the amount of fuel in the airplane prior to starting of engine. The figure obtained as a result of this computation will represent the amount of gasoline available and applicable for flight planning purposes on the RANGE IN AIR MILES section of the FLIGHT OPERATION INSTRUCTION CHART.

   (3) Select figure in fuel column equal to, or the next entry less than, available amount of fuel in airplane as determined in paragraph 2.a.(2) above. Move horizontally to right or left and select a figure equal to, or the next entry greater than, the air miles to be flown. Values contained in the column in which this figure appears, represent highest cruising speed possible at range desired; the airplane may be operated in accordance with values contained under OPERATING DATA in any column of a higher number with flight plan being completed at a sacrifice of speed but at greater fuel economy.

   (4) Using the same column number selected by application of instructions contained in paragraph 2.a.(3), determine the IAS and gallons per hour listed at sea level in the lower section of chart under subtitle OPERATING DATA. Divide this IAS into air miles to be flown and obtain the calculated flight duration in minutes, convert into hours and minutes and deduct from desired arrival time at destination in order to obtain the take-off time (without consideration for wind). To allow for wind, use the above IAS as ground speed and calculate a new corrected ground speed with the aid of a flight calculator or navigator's triangle of velocities.

   (5) Airplane and engine operating values listed below OPERATING DATA in any single numbered column are calculated to give constant miles per gallon at any altitude listed. Thus, airplane may be operated at any altitude and at the corresponding set of values given provided they are in the same column listing the range desired.

   CAUTION

   Ranges listed in column 1 under "Max Cont Power" are correct only at altitude given in footnote 1. Engine and airplane operating data listed under OPERATING DATA will give constant miles per gallon if operation is consistent with values set opposite listed altitudes.

   (6) Flight plan may be changed at any time en route, and the chart will show the balance of range at various cruising powers.

   b. If the original flight plan calls for a mission requiring changes in power, speed, gross load or external load, in accordance with "GR. WT." or "EXTERNAL ITEMS" increments shown in the series of "FLIGHT OPERATION INSTRUCTION CHARTS" provided, the total flight should be broken down into a series of individual short flights, each computed as outlined in paragraph 2.a. in its entirety, and then added together to make up the total flight and its requirements.

RESTRICTED   T. O. No. 01-115GA-1

WEIGHT & BALANCE CHART

SPEC. AN-H-8 DEC. 18, 1942   FORM ASC-513

AIRPLANE MODELS	CONDITION	CG LIMITS (IN INCHES) AFT OF REFERENCE DATUM LINE	
		F'W'D	AFT
....	TAKE-OFF	20% M.A.C.	....30%..
..........PT-19..............	LANDING	20% M.A.C.	....30%..

BASIC WEIGHT ITEMS	POUNDS
WEIGHT EMPTY (INCLUDING TRAPPED FUEL AND OIL)	1770
EQUIPMENT:	
NAVIGATION_____LB. PHOTOGRAPHIC_____LB. OXYGEN_____LB.	
PYROTECHNICS (FLARES, ETC.)_____LB.	
ARMAMENT:	
FIXED GUN INSTALLATION(S): ( )____CAL.____LB.; ( )____CAL.____LB.; GUN SIGHT____LB.	
FLEXIBLE GUN INSTALLATION(S): ( )____CAL.____LB.; ( )____CAL.____LB.	
CANNON INSTALLATION(S): ( )____MM.____LB.; ( )____MM.____LB.	
RADIO: MODEL(S)_____	
TOTAL BASIC WEIGHT (CG_____INCHES AFT OF REFERENCE DATUM LINE)	1770

ITEMS OF USEFUL LOAD	ALTERNATE LOADINGS (POUNDS)			
	MAXIMUM FUEL			
PILOT (200 LB. INCLUDING PARACHUTE)	200			
CREW (200 LB. EACH INCLUDING PARACHUTE) (Student)	200			
PASSENGERS (200 LB. EACH INCLUDING PARACHUTES)				
BAGGAGE (LB. MAXIMUM)				
FUEL (6 LB/U.S. GAL. OR 7.2 LB/IMP. GAL.): U.S. GAL. (IMP. GAL.)	270			
45 (37.4)				
( )				
( )				
( )				
( )				
OIL (7.5 LB/U.S. GAL. OR 9 LB/IMP. GAL.): 4.1 (3.4)	30			
( )				
EXTRA TANK(S) INSTALLATION				
BOMB INSTALLATION(S): ( ) INTERNAL AT_____LB. EACH				
( ) EXTERNAL AT_____LB. EACH				
TORPEDO INSTALLATION				
AMMUNITION				
( ) RD. OF_____CAL.; ( ) RD. OF_____CAL.				
( ) RD. OF_____MM.; ( ) RD. OF_____MM.				
NOTE: May be flown solo from either cockpit.				
GROSS WEIGHT	2470			
% M.A.C.	29.5			

RESTRICTED T. O. No. 01-115GA-1

WEIGHT & BALANCE CHART

SPEC. AN-H-8 DEC. 18, 1942
FORM ASC-513

AIRPLANE MODELS	CONDITION	CG LIMITS (IN INCHES) AFT OF REFERENCE DATUM LINE	
		F'W'D	AFT
....	TAKE-OFF	.20% M.A.C.	...30%...
..........PT-19A..........	LANDING	.20% M.A.C.	...30%...

BASIC WEIGHT ITEMS	POUNDS
WEIGHT EMPTY (INCLUDING TRAPPED FUEL AND OIL)	1820
EQUIPMENT:	
NAVIGATION_____LB. PHOTOGRAPHIC_____LB. OXYGEN_____LB.	
PYROTECHNICS (FLARES, ETC.)_____LB.	
ARMAMENT:	
FIXED GUN INSTALLATION(S): ( )____CAL.____LB.; ( )____CAL.____LB.; GUN SIGHT____LB.	
FLEXIBLE GUN INSTALLATION(S): ( )____CAL.____LB.; ( )____CAL.____LB.	
CANNON INSTALLATION(S): ( )____MM.____LB.; ( )____MM.____LB.	
RADIO: MODEL(S)_____	
TOTAL BASIC WEIGHT (CG_____INCHES AFT OF REFERENCE DATUM LINE)	1820

ITEMS OF USEFUL LOAD	ALTERNATE LOADINGS (POUNDS)			
	MAXIMUM FUEL			
PILOT (200 LB. INCLUDING PARACHUTE)	200			
CREW (200 LB. EACH INCLUDING PARACHUTE) (Student)	200			
PASSENGERS (200 LB. EACH INCLUDING PARACHUTES)				
BAGGAGE (____LB. MAXIMUM)				
FUEL (6 LB/U.S. GAL. OR 7.2 LB/IMP. GAL.): U.S. GAL. (IMP. GAL.)				
45 (37.4)	270			
( )				
( )				
( )				
( )				
OIL (7.5 LB/U.S. GAL. OR 9 LB/IMP. GAL.): 4.1 (3.4)	30			
( )				
EXTRA TANK(S) INSTALLATION				
BOMB INSTALLATION(S): ( ) INTERNAL AT_____LB. EACH				
( ) EXTERNAL AT_____LB. EACH				
TORPEDO INSTALLATION				
AMMUNITION				
( ) RD. OF_____CAL.; ( ) RD. OF_____CAL.				
( ) RD. OF_____MM.; ( ) RD. OF_____MM.				
NOTE: May be flown from either cockpit.				
GROSS WEIGHT	2520			
% M.A.C.	28.4			

RESTRICTED T. O. No. 01-115GA-1

WEIGHT & BALANCE CHART

SPEC. AN-H-8
DEC. 18, 1942
FORM ASC-513

AIRPLANE MODELS
....
.... PT-19B ....

CG LIMITS (IN INCHES) AFT OF REFERENCE DATUM LINE

CONDITION	F'W'D	AFT
TAKE-OFF	20% M.A.C.	30%
LANDING	20% M.A.C.	30%

BASIC WEIGHT ITEMS	POUNDS
WEIGHT EMPTY (INCLUDING TRAPPED FUEL AND OIL)	1940
EQUIPMENT:	
NAVIGATION ___ LB. PHOTOGRAPHIC ___ LB. OXYGEN ___ LB.	
PYROTECHNICS (FLARES, ETC.) ___ LB.	
ARMAMENT:	
FIXED GUN INSTALLATION(S): ( ) ___ CAL. ___ LB.; ( ) ___ CAL. ___ LB.; GUN SIGHT ___ LB.	
FLEXIBLE GUN INSTALLATION(S): ( ) ___ CAL. ___ LB.; ( ) ___ CAL. ___ LB.	
CANNON INSTALLATION(S): ( ) ___ MM. ___ LB.; ( ) ___ MM. ___ LB.	
RADIO: MODEL(S) ___	
TOTAL BASIC WEIGHT (CG ___ INCHES AFT OF REFERENCE DATUM LINE)	1940

ITEMS OF USEFUL LOAD	ALTERNATE LOADINGS (POUNDS)			
	MAXIMUM FUEL			
PILOT (200 LB. INCLUDING PARACHUTE)	200			
CREW (200 LB. EACH INCLUDING PARACHUTE) (Student)	200			
PASSENGERS (200 LB. EACH INCLUDING PARACHUTES)				
BAGGAGE (___ LB. MAXIMUM)				
FUEL (6 LB./U.S. GAL. OR 7.2 LB/IMP. GAL.): U.S. GAL. (IMP. GAL.)				
45 (37.4)	270			
( )				
( )				
( )				
( )				
OIL (7.5 LB/U.S. GAL. OR 9 LB/IMP. GAL.): 4.1 (3.4)	30			
( )				
EXTRA TANK(S) INSTALLATION				
BOMB INSTALLATION(S): ( ) INTERNAL AT ___ LB. EACH				
( ) EXTERNAL AT ___ LB. EACH				
TORPEDO INSTALLATION				
AMMUNITION				
( ) RD. OF ___ CAL.; ( ) RD. OF ___ CAL.				
( ) RD. OF ___ MM.; ( ) RD. OF ___ MM.				
NOTE: May be flown solo from either cockpit.				
GROSS WEIGHT	2640			
% M.A.C.	28.7			

SPEC. AN-H-8 DEC. 18, 1942
FORM ASC-513

WEIGHT & BALANCE CHART

AIRPLANE MODELS	CG LIMITS (IN INCHES) AFT OF REFERENCE DATUM LINE		
	CONDITION	F'W'D	AFT
....	TAKE-OFF	20% M.A.C.	30%
.......PT-23........	LANDING	20% M.A.C.	30%

BASIC WEIGHT ITEMS	POUNDS
WEIGHT EMPTY (INCLUDING TRAPPED FUEL AND OIL)	1970
EQUIPMENT:	
NAVIGATION_____LB. PHOTOGRAPHIC_____LB. OXYGEN_____LB.	
PYROTECHNICS (FLARES, ETC.)_____LB.	
ARMAMENT:	
FIXED GUN INSTALLATION(S): ( )_____CAL._____LB.; ( )_____CAL._____LB.; GUN SIGHT_____LB.	
FLEXIBLE GUN INSTALLATION(S): ( )_____CAL._____LB.; ( )_____CAL._____LB.	
CANNON INSTALLATION(S): ( )_____MM._____LB.; ( )_____MM._____LB.	
RADIO: MODEL(S)_____	
TOTAL BASIC WEIGHT (CG_____INCHES AFT OF REFERENCE DATUM LINE)	1970

ITEMS OF USEFUL LOAD	ALTERNATE LOADINGS (POUNDS)			
	MAXIMUM FUEL			
PILOT (200 LB. INCLUDING PARACHUTE)	200			
CREW (200 LB. EACH INCLUDING PARACHUTE) (Student)	200			
PASSENGERS (200 LB. EACH INCLUDING PARACHUTES)				
BAGGAGE (_____LB. MAXIMUM)				
FUEL (6 LB/U.S. GAL. OR 7.2 LB/IMP. GAL.): U.S. GAL. (IMP. GAL.)				
45 (37.4)	270			
( )				
( )				
( )				
( )				
OIL (7.5 LB/U.S. GAL. OR 9 LB/IMP. GAL.): 4.1 (3.4)	30			
( )				
EXTRA TANK(S) INSTALLATION				
BOMB INSTALLATION(S): ( ) INTERNAL AT_____LB. EACH				
( ) EXTERNAL AT_____LB. EACH				
TORPEDO INSTALLATION				
AMMUNITION				
( ) RD. OF_____CAL.; ( ) RD. OF_____CAL.				
( ) RD. OF_____MM.; ( ) RD. OF_____MM.				
NOTE: May be flown solo from either cockpit.				
GROSS WEIGHT	2670			
% M.A.C.	27.0			

RESTRICTED T. O. No. 01-115GA-1

WEIGHT & BALANCE CHART

SPEC. AN-H-8
DEC. 18, 1942
FORM ASC-513

AIRPLANE MODELS	CG LIMITS (IN INCHES) AFT OF REFERENCE DATUM LINE		
	CONDITION	F'W'D	AFT
....	TAKE-OFF	.20% M.A.C.	...30%...
........PT-26..........	LANDING	.20% M.A.C.	...30%...

BASIC WEIGHT ITEMS	POUNDS
WEIGHT EMPTY (INCLUDING TRAPPED FUEL AND OIL)	2010
EQUIPMENT:	
NAVIGATION_____LB. PHOTOGRAPHIC_____LB. OXYGEN_____LB.	
PYROTECHNICS (FLARES, ETC.)_____LB.	
ARMAMENT:	
FIXED GUN INSTALLATION(S): ( )____CAL.____LB.; ( )____CAL.____LB.; GUN SIGHT____LB.	
FLEXIBLE GUN INSTALLATION(S): ( )____CAL.____LB.; ( )____CAL.____LB.	
CANNON INSTALLATION(S): ( )____MM.____LB.; ( )____MM.____LB.	
RADIO: MODEL(S)_____	
TOTAL BASIC WEIGHT (CG_____INCHES AFT OF REFERENCE DATUM LINE)	2010

ITEMS OF USEFUL LOAD	ALTERNATE LOADINGS (POUNDS)			
	MAXIMUM FUEL			
PILOT (200 LB. INCLUDING PARACHUTE)	200			
CREW (200 LB. EACH INCLUDING PARACHUTE) (Student)	200			
PASSENGERS (200 LB. EACH INCLUDING PARACHUTES)				
BAGGAGE (____LB. MAXIMUM)				
FUEL (6 LB/U.S. GAL. OR 7.2 LB/IMP. GAL.): U.S. GAL. (IMP. GAL.)				
45 (37.4)	270			
( )				
( )				
( )				
( )				
OIL (7.5 LB/U.S. GAL. OR 9 LB/IMP. GAL.): 4.1 (3.4)	30			
( )				
EXTRA TANK(S) INSTALLATION				
BOMB INSTALLATION(S): ( ) INTERNAL AT____LB. EACH				
( ) EXTERNAL AT____LB. EACH				
TORPEDO INSTALLATION				
AMMUNITION				
( ) RD. OF____CAL.; ( ) RD. OF____CAL.				
( ) RD. OF____MM.; ( ) RD. OF____MM.				
NOTE: May be flown solo from either cockpit.				
GROSS WEIGHT	2710			
% M.A.C.	29.3			

RESTRICTED   T. O. No. 01-115GA-1

SPECIFIC ENGINE FLIGHT CHART

AIRPLANE MODELS: PT-19, PT-19A, PT-19B

ENGINE MODELS: L-440-1 (CONTRACTOR'S MODEL # 6-440C-2)

FORM ASC-512A

CONDITION	FUEL PRESSURE (LB/SQ. IN.)	OIL PRESSURE (LB/SQ. IN.)	OIL TEMP. °C	OIL TEMP. °F	COOLANT TEMP. °C	COOLANT TEMP. °F
DESIRED	3	60	71			
MAXIMUM	3.5	70	93			
MINIMUM	2.5	50	60			
IDLING	2.5	15				

MAX. PERMISSIBLE DIVING RPM: 2600

CONDITION	ALLOWABLE OIL CONSUMPTION		
NORMAL RATED (MAX. CONT.)	2.5 ... U.S.QT/HR	....	IMP.PT/HR
MAX. CRUISE	2.5 ... U.S.QT/HR	....	IMP.PT/HR
MIN. SPECIFIC	1.14 ... U.S.QT/HR	....	IMP.PT/HR
OIL GRADE: (S) .... 1120 .... (W) 1100			

SUPERCHARGER TYPE: **FUEL GRADE:** 73   **OCTANE**

OPERATING CONDITION	RPM	MANIFOLD PRESSURE (BOOST)	HORSE-POWER	CRITICAL ALTITUDE WITH RAM	CRITICAL ALTITUDE NO RAM	BLOWER USE LOW BLOWER BELOW:	MIXTURE CONTROL POSITION	FUEL FLOW (GAL./HR./ENG.) U.S.	FUEL FLOW IMP.	MAXIMUM CYL. TEMP. °C	MAXIMUM CYL. TEMP. °F	MAXIMUM DURATION (MINUTES)
TAKE-OFF	*FULL THROTTLE	FULL THROTTLE	*FULL THROTTLE	SEA LEVEL	SEA LEVEL		**FULL RICH	19		270	518	5 MINUTES
WAR EMERGENCY												
MILITARY												
NORMAL RATED (MAX. CONT.)	*FULL THROTTLE	FULL THROTTLE	*FULL THROTTLE	SEA LEVEL	SEA LEVEL		**FULL RICH	19		240	464	CONTINUOUS
MAXIMUM CRUISE	2230	PART THROTTLE	131		SEA LEVEL		**FULL RICH	13.5		240	464	CONTINUOUS
MINIMUM SPECIFIC CONSUMPTION	2065	PART THROTTLE	105		SEA LEVEL		PART LEAN	9.8		240	464	CONTINUOUS

REMARKS: * FULL THROTTLE = 175 HORSEPOWER AT 2450 R.P.M.

** USE FULL RICH MIXTURE UP TO 5000 FEET MANUAL LEAN ABOVE 5000 TO SMOOTH OPERATION.

Revised 5 August 1944   RESTRICTED

RESTRICTED   T. O. No. 01-115GA-1

SPECIFIC ENGINE FLIGHT CHART

AIRPLANE MODELS: PT-23

ENGINE MODELS: R-670-4, R-670-5, R-670-11

MAX. PERMISSIBLE DIVING RPM: 2490

CONDITION	ALLOWABLE OIL CONSUMPTION	
NORMAL RATED (MAX. CONT.)	3.0 U.S.QT/HR	IMP.PT/HR
MAX. CRUISE	2.5 U.S.QT/HR	IMP.PT/HR
MIN. SPECIFIC	2.5 U.S.QT/HR	IMP.PT/HR
OIL GRADE: (S) 1120	(W) 1100	

FUEL GRADE: 73 OCTANE

SUPERCHARGER TYPE:

CONDITION	FUEL PRESSURE (LB/SQ.IN.)	OIL PRESSURE (LB/SQ.IN.)	OIL TEMP. °C	OIL TEMP. °F	COOLANT TEMP. °C	COOLANT TEMP. °F
DESIRED	1.5 - 2	75	70			
MAXIMUM	2 - 5	90	95			
MINIMUM	1	60				
IDLING	1	30				

OPERATING CONDITION	RPM	MANIFOLD PRESSURE (BOOST)	HORSE-POWER	CRITICAL ALTITUDE WITH RAM	CRITICAL ALTITUDE NO RAM	BLOWER	USE LOW BLOWER BELOW:	MIXTURE CONTROL POSITION	FUEL FLOW (GAL/HR/ENG.) U.S.	FUEL FLOW IMP.	MAXIMUM CYL. TEMP. °C	MAXIMUM CYL. TEMP. °F	MAXIMUM DURATION (MINUTES)
TAKE-OFF	2075	F.T.	220	SEA LEVEL				*FULL RICH	21.3		260	526	5 MINUTES
WAR EMERGENCY													
MILITARY													
NORMAL RATED (MAX. CONT.)	2075	F.T.	220	SEA LEVEL				RICHEST SMOOTH OPERATION	21.3		260	526	CONT
MAXIMUM CRUISE	1890	P.T.	165	SEA LEVEL				*F.R.	18.		235	481	CONT
MINIMUM SPECIFIC CONSUMPTION	1800	P.T.	147	SEA LEVEL				MAXIMUM POWER	13.0		235	481	CONT

REMARKS: * USE FULL RICH MIXTURE UP TO 5000 FEET, HAND LEAN ABOVE 5000 FEET.

FORM ASC-512A

Revised 5 August 1944

RESTRICTED   T. O. No. 01-115GA-1

SPECIFIC ENGINE FLIGHT CHART

AIRPLANE MODELS: PT-26

ENGINE MODELS: L-440-3
(CONTRACTOR'S MODEL # 6-440C-5)

FORM ASC-512A

CONDITION	FUEL PRESSURE (LB/SQ. IN.)	OIL PRESSURE (LB/SQ. IN.)	OIL TEMP. °C	OIL TEMP. °F	COOLANT TEMP. °C	COOLANT TEMP. °F
DESIRED	3	60	71			
MAXIMUM	3.5	70	93			
MINIMUM	2.5	50	60			
IDLING	2.5	15				

SUPERCHARGER TYPE:

OPERATING CONDITION	RPM	MANIFOLD PRESSURE (BOOST)	HORSE-POWER	CRITICAL ALTITUDE WITH RAM	CRITICAL ALTITUDE NO RAM	BLOWER USE LOW BLOWER BELOW:	MIXTURE CONTROL POSITION	FUEL FLOW (GAL./HR/ENG.) U.S.	FUEL FLOW IMP.	MAXIMUM CYL. TEMP. °C	MAXIMUM CYL. TEMP. °F	MAXIMUM DURATION (MINUTES)
TAKE-OFF	*FULL THROTTLE	FULL THROTTLE	*FULL THROTTLE	SEA LEVEL	SEA LEVEL		**FULL RICH	19		270	518	5 MINUTES
WAR EMERGENCY												
MILITARY												
NORMAL RATED (MAX. CONT.)	*FULL THROTTLE	FULL THROTTLE	*FULL THROTTLE	SEA LEVEL	SEA LEVEL		**FULL RICH	19		240	464	CONTINUOUS
MAXIMUM CRUISE	2230	PART THROTTLE	150	SEA LEVEL	SEA LEVEL		**FULL RICH	13.5		240	464	CONTINUOUS
MINIMUM SPECIFIC CONSUMPTION	2065	PART THROTTLE	120	SEA LEVEL	SEA LEVEL		PART LEAN	9.8		240	464	CONTINUOUS

MAX. PERMISSIBLE DIVING RPM: 2600

ALLOWABLE OIL CONSUMPTION

CONDITION	U.S.QT/HR	IMP.PT/HR
NORMAL RATED (MAX. CONT.)	2.5	IMP.PT/HR
MAX. CRUISE	2.5	IMP.PT/HR
MIN. SPECIFIC	1.14	IMP.PT/HR

OIL GRADE: (S) 1120   (W) 1100

FUEL GRADE: 91 **OCTANE**

REMARKS: FULL THROTTLE = 200 H.P. AT 2450 R.P.M.
USE FULL RICH MIXTURE UP TO 5000 FEET HAND LEAN ABOVE 5000 FEET TO SMOOTH OPERATION.

Revised 5 August 1944   - 26 -   RESTRICTED

RESTRICTED   T. O. No. 01-115GA-1

AIRPLANE MODELS PT-19   **TAKE-OFF, CLIMB & LANDING CHART**   **ENGINE MODELS L-440-1**

TAKE-OFF DISTANCE (IN FEET)

GROSS WEIGHT (IN LBS.)	HEAD WIND (MPH)	HARD SURFACE RUNWAY							SOD-TURF RUNWAY							SOFT SURFACE RUNWAY						
		AT SEA LEVEL		AT 3,000 FT.		AT 6,000 FT.		AT SEA LEVEL		AT 3,000 FT.		AT 6,000 FT.		AT SEA LEVEL		AT 3,000 FT.		AT 6,000 FT.	
		GROUND RUN	TO CLEAR 50' OBJ.	GROUND RUN	TO CLEAR 50' OBJ.	GROUND RUN	TO CLEAR 50' OBJ.	GROUND RUN	TO CLEAR 50' OBJ.	GROUND RUN	TO CLEAR 50' OBJ.	GROUND RUN	TO CLEAR 50' OBJ.	GROUND RUN	TO CLEAR 50' OBJ.	GROUND RUN	TO CLEAR 50' OBJ.	GROUND RUN	TO CLEAR 50' OBJ.
2470 DUAL	0	800	1200	1100	1650	1600	2250	1300	1700	1800	2350	2600	3250	2600	3050	3600	4200	5300	6000
	20	450	750	600	1000	850	1400	700	1000	950	1400	1400	1900	1500	1750	2000	2400	2900	3400
	40	300	500	400	650	550	950	450	650	600	900	900	1250	900	1150	1500	1600	1800	2200
2270 SOLO	0	700	1050	950	1450	1350	2000	1100	1450	1500	2000	2200	2800	2200	2600	3100	3600	4500	5100
	20	400	650	500	850	750	1200	600	850	800	1200	1200	1650	1200	1500	1600	2000	2400	2900
	40	250	450	350	600	450	800	400	550	500	750	750	1100	800	1000	1100	1300	1500	1900

NOTE: INCREASE DISTANCE 10 % FOR EACH 10°C ABOVE 0°C (10 % FOR EACH 20 F ABOVE 32 F)   ENGINE LIMITS FOR TAKE-OFF   ✶ RPM & IN. HG

CLIMB DATA

COMBAT MISSIONS USE	TYPE OF CLIMB	✶ RPM			IN. HG	AT 6000				AT 9000				FERRY MISSIONS USE	AT 12000 FT.			RPM & FT. ALT.	IN. HG BLOWER CHANGE
GROSS WEIGHT (IN LBS.)		S.L. TO 3000 FT. ALT.			3000	6000				9000					BEST I.A.S.	TIME FROM S.L.	FUEL FROM S.L.		
		BEST I.A.S.	FT./MIN.	TIME FROM S.L.		BEST I.A.S.	FT./MIN.	TIME FROM S.L.	FUEL FROM S.L.	BEST I.A.S.	FT./MIN.	TIME FROM S.L.	FUEL FROM S.L.					
2470 DUAL	COMBAT FERRY	80	700	5		76	550	11	6.5	72	380	18	8.5		68	220	30	11
2270 SOLO	COMBAT FERRY	78	760	4.5	SAME AS COMBAT	74	600	10	(FULL THROTTLE RECOMMENDED DURING ALL CLIMBS)			66	240	27	
	COMBAT FERRY				SAME AS COMBAT				(FULL THROTTLE RECOMMENDED DURING ALL CLIMBS)							

NOTE: INCREASED ELAPSED CLIMBING TIME 5 % FOR EACH 10°C ABOVE 0°C FREE AIR TEMPERATURE (5 % FOR EACH 20 F ABOVE 32 F)   FUEL INCLUDES WARM-UP AND TAKE-OFF ALLOWANCE

LANDING DISTANCE (IN FEET)

GROSS WEIGHT (IN LBS.)	BEST I.A.S.	HARD DRY SURFACE						FIRM DRY SOD						WET OR SLIPPERY					
		AT SEA LEVEL		AT 3,000 FT.		AT 6,000 FT.		AT SEA LEVEL		AT 3,000 FT.		AT 6,000 FT.		AT SEA LEVEL		AT 3,000 FT.		AT 6,000 FT.	
	Approach	TO CLEAR 50' OBJ.	GROUND ROLL	TO CLEAR 50' OBJ.	GROUND ROLL	TO CLEAR 50' OBJ.	GROUND ROLL	TO CLEAR 50' OBJ.	GROUND ROLL	TO CLEAR 50' OBJ.	GROUND ROLL	TO CLEAR 50' OBJ.	GROUND ROLL	TO CLEAR 50' OBJ.	GROUND ROLL	TO CLEAR 50' OBJ.	GROUND ROLL	TO CLEAR 50' OBJ.	GROUND ROLL
2470	80	650	550	1150	1050	1250	1100	900	700	1450	1200	1550	1300	1900	1600	2350	2050	2600	2300
2270	75	1100	1000			800	650	1350	1150	1000	750	1100	850			2100	1750	2800	2400

NOTE: FOR GROUND TEMPERATURES ABOVE 35°C (95°F) INCREASE APPROACH I.A.S. 10% AND ALLOW 20% INCREASE IN GROUND ROLL.

REMARKS ✶ FULL THROTTLE

LEGEND
I.A.S.: Indicated Air Speed
NOTE: All distances are average, and subject to considerable variations, because of differences in pilot technique, load, C.G., etc.
RED FIGURES HAVE NOT BEEN FLIGHT CHECKED.

Revised 25 May 1944   - 27 -   RESTRICTED

RESTRICTED T. O. No. 01-115GA-1

TAKE-OFF, CLIMB & LANDING CHART

AIRPLANE MODELS PT-19A
ENGINE MODELS L-440-1

TAKE-OFF DISTANCE (IN FEET)

GROSS WEIGHT (IN LBS.)	HEAD WIND (MPH)	HARD SURFACE RUNWAY						SOD-TURF RUNWAY						SOFT SURFACE RUNWAY					
		AT SEA LEVEL		AT 3,000 FT.		AT 6,000 FT.		AT SEA LEVEL		AT 3,000 FT.		AT 6,000 FT.		AT SEA LEVEL		AT 3,000 FT.		AT 6,000 FT.	
		GROUND RUN	TO CLEAR 50' OBJ.	GROUND RUN	TO CLEAR 50' OBJ.	GROUND RUN	TO CLEAR 50' OBJ.	GROUND RUN	TO CLEAR 50' OBJ.	GROUND RUN	TO CLEAR 50' OBJ.	GROUND RUN	TO CLEAR 50' OBJ.	GROUND RUN	TO CLEAR 50' OBJ.	GROUND RUN	TO CLEAR 50' OBJ.	GROUND RUN	TO CLEAR 50' OBJ.
2520 DUAL	0	800	1200	1100	1650	1600	2250	1300	1700	1800	2350	2600	3250	2600	3050	3600	4200	5300	6000
	20	450	750	600	1000	850	1400	700	1000	950	1400	1600	1900	1500	1750	2000	2400	2900	3400
	40	300	500	400	650	550	950	450	650	600	900	900	1250	1000	1150	1500	1800	1800	2200
2320 SOLO	0	700	1050	950	1450	1350	2000	1100	1450	1500	2000	2200	2800	2200	2600	3100	3600	4500	5100
	20	400	650	500	850	750	1200	600	850	800	1200	1200	1650	1200	1500	1600	2000	2400	2900
	40	250	450	350	600	450	800	400	550	500	750	750	1100	800	1000	1100	1300	1500	1900

NOTE: INCREASE DISTANCE 10 % FOR EACH 10 C ABOVE 0 C (10 % FOR EACH 20 F ABOVE 32 F) ENGINE LIMITS FOR TAKE-OFF ___ RPM & ___ IN. HG.

CLIMB DATA

COMBAT MISSIONS USE ✱		S.L. TO 3000 FT. ALT.			AT 3000 FT. ALT.				AT 6000 FT. ALT.				AT 9000 FT. ALT.				FERRY MISSIONS USE AT 12000 FT. ALT.				RPM & ___ IN. HG.
GROSS WEIGHT (IN LBS.)	TYPE OF CLIMB	BEST I.A.S.	FT./MIN.	TIME FROM S.L.	BEST I.A.S.	FT./MIN.	TIME FROM S.L.	FUEL FROM S.L.	BEST I.A.S.	FT./MIN.	TIME FROM S.L.	FUEL FROM S.L.	BEST I.A.S.	FT./MIN.	TIME FROM S.L.	FUEL FROM S.L.	BEST I.A.S.	FT./MIN.	TIME FROM S.L.	FUEL FROM S.L.	BLOWER CHANGE
2520 DUAL	COMBAT FERRY	80	700	5	76	550	11	6.5	72	380	18	8.5	68	220	30	11					
2320 SOLO	COMBAT FERRY	78	760	4.5	74	600	10	SAME AS COMBAT	70	410	16	(FULL THROTTLE RECOMMENDED DURING ALL CLIMBS)	66	240	27	(FULL THROTTLE RECOMMENDED DURING ALL CLIMBS)					
	COMBAT FERRY																				

NOTE: INCREASED ELAPSED CLIMBING TIME 5 % FOR EACH 10°C ABOVE 0°C FREE AIR TEMPERATURE (5 % FOR EACH 20°F ABOVE 32°F) FUEL INCLUDES WARM-UP AND TAKE-OFF ALLOWANCE

LANDING DISTANCE (IN FEET)

GROSS WEIGHT (IN LBS.)	BEST I.A.S. Approach	HARD DRY SURFACE						FIRM DRY SOD						WET OR SLIPPERY					
		AT SEA LEVEL		AT 3,000 FT.		AT 6,000 FT.		AT SEA LEVEL		AT 3,000 FT.		AT 6,000 FT.		AT SEA LEVEL		AT 3,000 FT.		AT 6,000 FT.	
		TO CLEAR 50' OBJ.	GROUND ROLL	TO CLEAR 50' OBJ.	GROUND ROLL	TO CLEAR 50' OBJ.	GROUND ROLL	TO CLEAR 50' OBJ.	GROUND ROLL	TO CLEAR 50' OBJ.	GROUND ROLL	TO CLEAR 50' OBJ.	GROUND ROLL	TO CLEAR 50' OBJ.	GROUND ROLL	TO CLEAR 50' OBJ.	GROUND ROLL	TO CLEAR 50' OBJ.	GROUND ROLL
2520	80	1100	650	1150	700	1250	800	1350	900	1450	1000	1550	1100	2350	1900	2600	2100	2800	2300
2320	75	1000	550	1050	600	1150	650	1150	700	1200	750	1300	850	2050	1600	2200	1750	2400	1900

NOTE: FOR GROUND TEMPERATURES ABOVE 35°C (95°F) INCREASE APPROACH I.A.S. 10% AND ALLOW 20% INCREASE IN GROUND ROLL.

REMARKS ✱ FULL THROTTLE

LEGEND
I.A.S.: Indicated Air Speed
NOTE: All distances are average, and subject to considerable variations because of differences in pilot technique, load, C.G., etc.
RED FIGURES HAVE NOT BEEN FLIGHT CHECKED.

Revised 25 May 1944 - 28 - RESTRICTED

RESTRICTED T. O. No. 01-115GA-1

AIRPLANE MODELS: PT-19B
TAKE-OFF, CLIMB & LANDING CHART
ENGINE MODELS: L-440-1

TAKE-OFF DISTANCE (IN FEET)

GROSS WEIGHT (IN LBS.)	HEAD WIND (MPH)	HARD SURFACE RUNWAY							SOD-TURF RUNWAY							SOFT SURFACE RUNWAY						
		AT SEA LEVEL		AT 3,000 FT.		AT 6,000 FT.		AT SEA LEVEL		AT 3,000 FT.		AT 6,000 FT.		AT SEA LEVEL		AT 3,000 FT.		AT 6,000 FT.	
		GROUND RUN	TO CLEAR 50' OBJ.	GROUND RUN	TO CLEAR 50' OBJ.	GROUND RUN	TO CLEAR 50' OBJ.	GROUND RUN	TO CLEAR 50' OBJ.	GROUND RUN	TO CLEAR 50' OBJ.	GROUND RUN	TO CLEAR 50' OBJ.	GROUND RUN	TO CLEAR 50' OBJ.	GROUND RUN	TO CLEAR 50' OBJ.	GROUND RUN	TO CLEAR 50' OBJ.
2640 DUAL	0	800	1200	1100	1650	1600	2250	1300	1700	1800	2350	2600	3250	2600	3050	3600	4200	5300	6000
	20	450	750	600	1000	850	1400	700	1000	950	1400	1400	1900	1500	1750	2000	2400	2900	3400
	40	300	500	400	650	550	950	450	650	600	900	900	1250	900	1150	1500	1600	1800	2200
2440 SOLO	0	700	1050	950	1450	1350	2000	1100	1450	1500	2000	2200	2800	2200	2600	3100	3600	4500	5100
	20	400	650	500	850	750	1200	600	850	800	1200	1200	1650	1200	1500	1600	2000	2400	2900
	40	250	450	350	600	450	800	400	550	500	750	750	1100	800	1000	1100	1300	1500	1900

NOTE: INCREASE DISTANCE 10 % FOR EACH 10 C ABOVE 0 C (10 % FOR EACH 20 F ABOVE 32 F) ENGINE LIMITS FOR TAKE-OFF *   IN. HG

CLIMB DATA

COMBAT MISSIONS USE *	TYPE OF CLIMB	S.L. TO 3000 FT. ALT.			AT 3000 FT. ALT.	RPM & IN. HG	AT 6000 FT. ALT.			AT 9000 FT. ALT.			FERRY MISSIONS USE *	AT 12000 FT. ALT.			RPM & IN. HG
GROSS WEIGHT (IN LBS.)		BEST I.A.S.	FT./MIN.	TIME FROM S.L.			BEST I.A.S.	FT./MIN.	TIME FROM S.L.	BEST I.A.S.	FT./MIN.	TIME FROM S.L.		BEST I.A.S.	FT./MIN.	TIME FROM S.L. FUEL	BLOWER CHANGE
2640 DUAL	COMBAT FERRY	80	700	5	76 550 11 6.5		72	380	18 8.5	68	220	30 11					
2440 SOLO	COMBAT FERRY	78	760	4.5	SAME AS COMBAT (FULL THROTTLE RECOMMENDED DURING ALL CLIMBS)		74	600	10	70	410	16		66	240	27	
	COMBAT FERRY				SAME AS COMBAT (FULL THROTTLE RECOMMENDED DURING ALL CLIMBS)												

NOTE: INCREASED ELAPSED CLIMBING TIME 5 % FOR EACH 10°C ABOVE 0 C FREE AIR TEMPERATURE (5 % FOR EACH 20 F ABOVE 32 F)   FUEL INCLUDES WARM-UP AND TAKE-OFF ALLOWANCE

LANDING DISTANCE (IN FEET)

GROSS WEIGHT (IN LBS.)	BEST I.A.S. Approach	HARD DRY SURFACE						FIRM DRY SOD						WET OR SLIPPERY					
		AT SEA LEVEL		AT 3,000 FT.		AT 6,000 FT.		AT SEA LEVEL		AT 3,000 FT.		AT 6,000 FT.		AT SEA LEVEL		AT 3,000 FT.		AT 6,000 FT.	
		GROUND ROLL	TO CLEAR 50' OBJ.	GROUND ROLL	TO CLEAR 50' OBJ.	GROUND ROLL	TO CLEAR 50' OBJ.	GROUND ROLL	TO CLEAR 50' OBJ.	GROUND ROLL	TO CLEAR 50' OBJ.	GROUND ROLL	TO CLEAR 50' OBJ.	GROUND ROLL	TO CLEAR 50' OBJ.	GROUND ROLL	TO CLEAR 50' OBJ.	GROUND ROLL	TO CLEAR 50' OBJ.
2640	80	650	1100	700	1150	700	1250	900	1350	1000	1450	1100	1550	1900	2350	2100	2600	2300	2800
2440	75	550	1000	600	1050	650	1100	750	1150	1200	1450	850	1300	1600	2050	1750	2200	1900	2400

NOTE: FOR GROUND TEMPERATURES ABOVE 35°C (95°F) INCREASE APPROACH I.A.S. 10% AND ALLOW 20% INCREASE IN GROUND ROLL.

REMARKS
*FULL THROTTLE

LEGEND
I.A.S.: Indicated Air Speed
NOTE: All distances are average, and subject to considerable variations because of differences in pilot technique, load, C.G., etc.
RED FIGURES HAVE NOT BEEN FLIGHT CHECKED.

Revised 25 May 1944

RESTRICTED   T. O. No. 01-115GA-1

AIRPLANE MODELS PT-23
TAKE-OFF, CLIMB & LANDING CHART
ENGINE MODELS R-670-4

TAKE-OFF DISTANCE (IN FEET)

GROSS WEIGHT (IN LBS.)	HEAD WIND (MPH)	HARD SURFACE RUNWAY							SOD-TURF RUNWAY							SOFT SURFACE RUNWAY						
		AT SEA LEVEL		AT 3,000 FT.		AT 6,000 FT.		AT SEA LEVEL		AT 3,000 FT.		AT 6,000 FT.		AT SEA LEVEL		AT 3,000 FT.		AT 6,000 FT.	
		GROUND RUN	TO CLEAR 50' OBJ.	GROUND RUN	TO CLEAR 50' OBJ.	GROUND RUN	TO CLEAR 50' OBJ.	GROUND RUN	TO CLEAR 50' OBJ.	GROUND RUN	TO CLEAR 50' OBJ.	GROUND RUN	TO CLEAR 50' OBJ.	GROUND RUN	TO CLEAR 50' OBJ.	GROUND RUN	TO CLEAR 50' OBJ.	GROUND RUN	TO CLEAR 50' OBJ.
2660 DUAL	0	800	1200	875	1300	950	1380	1300	1700	1450	1875	1550	1980	2600	3000	2900	3325	3100	3530
	20	410	600	450	650	500	710	650	840	750	950	800	1010	1350	1540	1500	1700	1650	1860
	40	250	370	270	400	300	430	400	520	450	580	500	630	800	920	900	1030	1000	1130
2460 SOLO	0	700	1060	750	1120	800	1160	1150	1510	1250	1620	1300	1660	2300	2660	2500	2870	2600	2960
	20	350	520	380	550	430	610	550	720	600	770	700	880	1150	1320	1250	1420	1400	1580
	40	220	330	230	340	260	370	350	460	400	510	400	510	700	810	750	860	850	960

NOTE: INCREASE DISTANCE 10 % FOR EACH 10 C ABOVE 0 C (10 % FOR EACH 20 F ABOVE 32 F)
ENGINE LIMITS FOR TAKE-OFF ✶ RPM & ✶ IN. HG

CLIMB DATA

COMBAT MISSIONS USE			✶ RPM & IN. HG			FERRY MISSIONS USE			✶ RPM & IN. HG		
GROSS WEIGHT (IN LBS.)	TYPE OF CLIMB	BEST I.A.S.	S.L. TO 3000 FT. ALT.		AT 6000 FT. ALT.		AT 9000 FT. ALT.		AT 12000 FT. ALT.		BLOWER CHANGE
			FT./MIN	TIME FROM S.L.	FT./MIN	TIME FROM S.L.	FT./MIN	TIME FROM S.L.	FT./MIN	TIME FROM S.L.	
2660 DUAL	COMBAT FERRY	80	870	4	670	9	470	15	280	26	
2460 SOLO	COMBAT FERRY	78	980	3.5	780	7	580	12.5	370	21	
	COMBAT FERRY		SAME AS COMBAT		SAME AS COMBAT		(FULL THROTTLE RECOMMENDED DURING ALL CLIMBS)				

NOTE: INCREASED ELAPSED CLIMBING TIME 5 % FOR EACH 10°C ABOVE 0°C FREE AIR TEMPERATURE (5 % FOR EACH 20 F ABOVE 32 F)
FUEL INCLUDES WARM-UP AND TAKE-OFF ALLOWANCE

LANDING DISTANCE (IN FEET)

GROSS WEIGHT (IN LBS.)	BEST I.A.S. Approach	HARD DRY SURFACE						FIRM DRY SOD						WET OR SLIPPERY					
		AT SEA LEVEL		AT 3,000 FT.		AT 6,000 FT.		AT SEA LEVEL		AT 3,000 FT.		AT 6,000 FT.		AT SEA LEVEL		AT 3,000 FT.		AT 6,000 FT.	
		TO CLEAR 50' OBJ.	GROUND ROLL	TO CLEAR 50' OBJ.	GROUND ROLL	TO CLEAR 50' OBJ.	GROUND ROLL	TO CLEAR 50' OBJ.	GROUND ROLL	TO CLEAR 50' OBJ.	GROUND ROLL	TO CLEAR 50' OBJ.	GROUND ROLL	TO CLEAR 50' OBJ.	GROUND ROLL	TO CLEAR 50' OBJ.	GROUND ROLL	TO CLEAR 50' OBJ.	GROUND ROLL
2660	80	1100	750	1170	820	1250	900	1350	1000	1450	1100	1550	1200	2350	2000	2650	2300	2850	2500
2460	77	1000	650	1070	720	1150	800	1150	800	1250	900	1350	1000	1950	1600	2250	1900	2450	2100

NOTE: FOR GROUND TEMPERATURES ABOVE 35°C (95°F) INCREASE APPROACH I.A.S. 10% AND ALLOW 20% INCREASE IN GROUND ROLL.

REMARKS ✶ FULL THROTTLE

LEGEND
I.A.S.: Indicated Air Speed
NOTE: All distances are average, and subject to considerable variations because of differences in pilot technique, load, C.G., etc.
RED FIGURES HAVE NOT BEEN FLIGHT CHECKED.

Revised 25 May 1944   - 30 -   RESTRICTED

RESTRICTED T. O. No. 01-115GA-1

AIRPLANE MODELS PT-26

TAKE-OFF, CLIMB & LANDING CHART

ENGINE MODELS L-440-3, -7

TAKE-OFF DISTANCE (IN FEET)

GROSS WEIGHT (IN LBS.)	HEAD WIND (MPH)	HARD SURFACE RUNWAY							SOD-TURF RUNWAY							SOFT SURFACE RUNWAY						
		AT SEA LEVEL		AT 3,000 FT.		AT 6,000 FT.		AT SEA LEVEL		AT 3,000 FT.		AT 6,000 FT.		AT SEA LEVEL		AT 3,000 FT.		AT 6,000 FT.	
		GROUND RUN	TO CLEAR 50' OBJ.	GROUND RUN	TO CLEAR 50' OBJ.	GROUND RUN	TO CLEAR 50' OBJ.	GROUND RUN	TO CLEAR 50' OBJ.	GROUND RUN	TO CLEAR 50' OBJ.	GROUND RUN	TO CLEAR 50' OBJ.	GROUND RUN	TO CLEAR 50' OBJ.	GROUND RUN	TO CLEAR 50' OBJ.	GROUND RUN	TO CLEAR 50' OBJ.
2650 DUAL	0	800	1200	1300		950	1380	1300	1700	450	875	550	980	2600	3000	2900	3325	3100	3530
	20	410	600	650		500	710	650	840	750	950	800	1010	1350	1540	1550	1700	1650	1860
	40	250	370	400		300	430	400	520	450	580	500	630	800	920	900	1030	1000	1130
2450 SOLO	0	700	1060	1120		800	1160	1150	1510	1250	1620	1300	1660	2300	2660	2500	2870	2600	2960
	20	350	520	550		430	610	550	720	600	770	700	880	1150	1320	1250	1420	1400	1580
	40	220	330	340		260	370	350	460	400	510	400	510	700	810	750	860	850	960

NOTE: INCREASE DISTANCE 10 % FOR EACH 10 C ABOVE 0 C (10 % FOR EACH 20 F ABOVE 32 F) ENGINE LIMITS FOR TAKE-OFF ✱ _____ RPM & _____ IN. HG

CLIMB DATA

COMBAT MISSIONS USE ✱	TYPE OF CLIMB	RPM & _____ IN. HG				3000 FT. ALT.		6000 FT. ALT.		9000 FT. ALT.		FERRY MISSIONS USE ✱	12000 FT. ALT.		RPM & _____ IN. HG	FT. ALT.	BLOWER CHANGE
		S.L. TO 3000 FT. ALT.			BEST I.A.S.	TIME FROM S.L.	BEST I.A.S.	TIME FROM S.L.	BEST I.A.S.	TIME FROM S.L.	BEST I.A.S.	TIME FROM S.L.	FUEL FROM S.L.			
		BEST I.A.S.	FT./MIN.	TIME FROM S.L.		FT./MIN.		FT./MIN.		FT./MIN.	FUEL FROM S.L.		FT./MIN.			
2650 DUAL	COMBAT FERRY	82	640	5	78	540	11	75	440	18	71	340	26	9.8			
2450 SOLO	COMBAT FERRY	80	720	4.5	76	630	9	73	540	15	69	450	22	8.8			
	COMBAT FERRY	SAME AS COMBAT			SAME AS COMBAT		(FULL THROTTLE RECOMMENDED DURING ALL CLIMBS)											

NOTE: INCREASED ELAPSED CLIMBING TIME 5 % FOR EACH 10°C ABOVE 0°C FREE AIR TEMPERATURE (5 % FOR EACH 20 F ABOVE 32°F) FUEL INCLUDES WARM-UP AND TAKE-OFF ALLOWANCE

LANDING DISTANCE (IN FEET)

GROSS WEIGHT (IN LBS.)	BEST I.A.S. Approach	HARD DRY SURFACE						FIRM DRY SOD						WET OR SLIPPERY					
		AT SEA LEVEL		AT 3,000 FT.		AT 6,000 FT.		AT SEA LEVEL		AT 3,000 FT.		AT 6,000 FT.		AT SEA LEVEL		AT 3,000 FT.		AT 6,000 FT.	
		TO CLEAR 50' OBJ.	GROUND ROLL	TO CLEAR 50' OBJ.	GROUND ROLL	TO CLEAR 50' OBJ.	GROUND ROLL	TO CLEAR 50' OBJ.	GROUND ROLL	TO CLEAR 50' OBJ.	GROUND ROLL	TO CLEAR 50' OBJ.	GROUND ROLL	TO CLEAR 50' OBJ.	GROUND ROLL	TO CLEAR 50' OBJ.	GROUND ROLL	TO CLEAR 50' OBJ.	GROUND ROLL
2650	78	1100	750	1170	820	1250	900	1350	1000	1450	1100	1550	1200	2350	2000	2650	2300	2850	2500
2250	76	1000	650	1070	720	1150	800	1150	900	1250	1000	1350	1000	1950	1600	2250	1900	2450	2100

NOTE: FOR GROUND TEMPERATURES ABOVE 35°C (95°F) INCREASE APPROACH I.A.S. 10% AND ALLOW 20% INCREASE IN GROUND ROLL.

REMARKS ✱ FULL THROTTLE

LEGEND

I.A.S.: Indicated Air Speed

NOTE: All distances are average, and subject to considerable variations, because of differences in pilot technique, load, C.G., etc. RED FIGURES HAVE NOT BEEN FLIGHT CHECKED.

Revised 25 May 1944

RESTRICTED T. O. No. 01-115GA-1

FLIGHT OPERATION INSTRUCTION CHART

MODEL(S): PT-19, PT-19A
ENGINE(S): L-440-1
CHART WEIGHT LIMITS: 2140 to 2518 POUNDS
EXTERNAL LOAD ITEMS: NONE

LIMITS:
	R.P.M.	M.P. (IN. HG.)	BLOWER POSITION	MIXTURE POSITION	TIME LIMIT	TOTAL G.P.H.
WAR MAX.						
MILITARY POWER						
NORMAL RATED	2450			F.R.	CONT.	18.5

NOTES: Column I is for emergency high speed cruising only. Columns II, III, IV and V give progressive increase in range at a sacrifice in speed. Manifold pressure (M. P.), gallons per hour (G. P. H.) and true airspeed (T. A. S.) are approximate values for reference. For efficiency maintain indicated airspeed (I. A. S.) hourly. Adjust RPM slightly if necessary to avoid exceeding manifold pressure more than 3 in. Hg.

INSTRUCTIONS FOR USING CHART: Select figure in FUEL column equal to or less than amount of fuel to be used for cruising. Move horizontally to left or right and select RANGE value equal to or greater than the statute or nautical air miles to be flown. Vertically below and opposite desired cruising altitude (ALT.) read optimum R. P. M., I. A. S. and MIXTURE setting required.

Range Table

I RANGE (STATUTE)	I RANGE (NAUTICAL)	II RANGE (STATUTE)	II RANGE (NAUTICAL)	FUEL U.S. GAL.	III RANGE (STATUTE)	III RANGE (NAUTICAL)	IV RANGE (STATUTE)	IV RANGE (NAUTICAL)	FUEL U.S. GAL.	V RANGE (STATUTE)	V RANGE (NAUTICAL)
240	210	300	260	40	320	280	340	295	40	380	330
210	180	265	230	35	280	245	300	260	35	335	290
180	155	225	195	30	240	210	255	220	30	285	250
150	130	190	165	25	200	175	210	180	25	240	210
120	105	150	130	20	160	140	170	150	20	190	165
90	80	115	100	15	120	105	130	115	15	145	125
60	50	75	65	10	80	70	85	75	10	95	85

Operating Data

MAXIMUM CONTINUOUS

R.P.M.	I.A.S. M.P.H.	MIX- TURE	M.P. In. Hg.	G. P. H.	T. A. S.	ALT. Feet	R.P.M.	I.A.S. M.P.H.	MIX- TURE	M.P. In. Hg.	G. P. H.	T. A. S.	R.P.M.	I.A.S. M.P.H.	MIX- TURE	M.P. In. Hg.	G. P. H.	T. A. S.	R.P.M.	I.A.S. M.P.H.	MIX- TURE	M.P. In. Hg.	G. P. H.	T. A. S.
						40000																		
						35000																		
						30000																		
						25000																		
						20000																		
						9000																		
						6000	2375	109	P.L.															
						3000	2280	111	F.R.	15.6			2280	119	F.R.	13.6								
2450	124	F.R.		18.5	124	S.L.	2150	109	F.R.	13.6			2100	108	F.R.	2.2			2100	106	F.R.			

MAXIMUM RANGE

R.P.M.	I.A.S. M.P.H.	MIX- TURE	M.P. In. Hg.	G. P. H.	T. A. S.
2270	99	P.L.		1.2	14
2175	99	P.L.			
2090	101	F.R.	0.4	09	
1970	99	F.R.	0.5	06	
			9.4	99	

NOTES:
○ ALLOW 5 GAL. FOR WARM-UP, TAKE-OFF & INITIAL CLIMB PLUS ALLOWANCE FOR WIND, RESERVE & COMBAT AS REQ'D.

EXAMPLE: AT 2500 LB GROSS WT. WITH 33 GAL. OF FUEL (AFTER DEDUCTING TOTAL ALLOWANCES OF 12 GAL.) TO FLY 230 STAT. AIRMILES AT 6000 FT. ALT. MAINTAIN 2325 RPM AND 107 MPH IND. AIRSPEED WITH MIXTURE SET P. L.

LEGEND
I.A.S.: INDICATED AIRSPEED
M.P.: MANIFOLD PRESSURE
G.P.H.: U.S. GAL. PER HOUR
T.A.S.: TRUE AIRSPEED
S.L.: SEA LEVEL
P.L.: PART LEAN
F.T.: FULL THROTTLE
F.R.: FULL RICH
A.R.: AUTO-RICH
A.L.: AUTO-LEAN
C.L.: CRUISING LEAN

RED FIGURES ARE PRELIMINARY, SUBJECT TO REVISION AFTER FLIGHT CHECK

Revised 25 May 1944 — 32 — RESTRICTED

RESTRICTED   T. O. No. 01-115GA-1

FLIGHT OPERATION INSTRUCTION CHART

MODEL(S): PT-19B
ENGINE(S): L-440-1

EXTERNAL LOAD ITEMS: NONE

CHART WEIGHT LIMITS: 2225 TO 2615 POUNDS

LIMITS	R.P.M.	M.P. (IN. HG.)	BLOWER POSITION	MIXTURE POSITION	TIME LIMIT	TOTAL G.P.H.
WAR MAX.						
MILITARY POWER						
NORMAL RATED	2450			F.R.	CONT.	18.5

INSTRUCTIONS FOR USING CHART: Select figure in FUEL column equal to or less than amount of fuel to be used for cruising. Move horizontally to left or right and select RANGE value equal to or greater than the statute or nautical air miles to be flown. Vertically below and opposite desired cruising altitude (ALT.) read optimum R.P.M., I.A.S. and MIXTURE setting required.

NOTES: Column I is for emergency high speed cruising only. Columns II, III, IV and V give progressive increase in range at a sacrifice in speed. Manifold pressure (M. P.), gallons per hour (G. P. H.) and true airspeed (T. A. S.) are approximate values for reference. For efficiency maintain indicated airspeed (I. A. S.) hourly. Adjust RPM slightly if necessary to avoid exceeding manifold pressure more than 3 in. Hg.

MAXIMUM CONTINUOUS — I

RANGE IN AIR MILES		FUEL U.S. GAL.	ALT. Feet	RANGE IN AIR MILES — II			RANGE IN AIR MILES — III			RANGE IN AIR MILES — IV			FUEL U.S. GAL.	RANGE IN AIR MILES — V	
STATUTE	NAUTICAL			STATUTE	NAUTICAL		STATUTE	NAUTICAL		STATUTE	NAUTICAL			STATUTE	NAUTICAL
		40	40000										40		
		35	35000										35		
240	210	30	30000	290	250		310	270		320	280		30	360	315
180	155	25	25000	255	220		270	235		285	250		25	315	275
150	130	20	20000	220	190		230	200		245	215		20	270	235
120	105	15	9000	180	155		195	170		205	180		20	225	195
90	80	15	6000	145	125		155	135		160	140		15	180	155
60	50	10	3000	110	95		115	100		125	110		15	135	115
			S.L.	75	.65		80	70		80	70		10	90	80

OPERATING DATA

R.P.M.	MIX. TURE	I.A.S. M.P.H.	M.P. In. Hg.	G.P.H.	T.A.S.		R.P.M.	MIX. TURE	I.A.S. M.P.H.	M.P. In. Hg.	G.P.H.	T.A.S.		R.P.M.	MIX. TURE	I.A.S. M.P.H.	M.P. In. Hg.	G.P.H.	T.A.S.		R.P.M.	MIX. TURE	I.A.S. M.P.H.	M.P. In. Hg.	G.P.H.	T.A.S.		R.P.M.	MIX. TURE	I.A.S. M.P.H.	M.P. In. Hg.	G.P.H.	T.A.S.
2450	F.R.	123		18.5	123		2400	F.R.	117	15.7		110		2350	F.R.	114	105				2375	F.R.	109		13.8	120		2350	P.L.	102			
							2230	F.R.	110	13.6				2150	F.R.	105	22				2280	F.R.	110	14.6		119		2260	P.L.	104			
																					2100	F.R.	102	2.2	13.2	115		2170	F.R.	104			94
																									11.3	102		1970	F.R.	94		9.4	94

NOTES

○ ALLOW 5 GAL. FOR WARM-UP, TAKE-OFF & INITIAL CLIMB PLUS ALLOWANCE FOR WIND, RESERVE & COMBAT AS REQ'D.

EXAMPLE

AT 2615 LB. GROSS WT. WITH 36 GAL. OF FUEL (AFTER DEDUCTING TOTAL ALLOWANCES OF 9 GAL.) TO FLY 250 STAT. AIRMILES AT 6000 FT. ALT. MAINTAIN 2375 RPM AND 109 MPH IND. AIRSPEED WITH MIXTURE SET P.L.

LEGEND

I.A.S.: INDICATED AIRSPEED   F.T.: FULL THROTTLE
M.P.: MANIFOLD PRESSURE   F.R.: FULL RICH
G.P.H.: U.S. GAL. PER HOUR   A.R.: AUTO-RICH
T.A.S.: TRUE AIRSPEED   A.L.: AUTO-LEAN
S.L.: SEA LEVEL   C.L.: CRUISING LEAN
   P.L.: PART LEAN

RED FIGURES ARE PRELIMINARY, SUBJECT TO REVISION AFTER FLIGHT CHECK.

Revised 25 May 1944   RESTRICTED

RESTRICTED T. O. No. 01-115GA-1

FLIGHT OPERATION INSTRUCTION CHART

MODEL(S): PT-23
ENGINE(S): R-670-4
CHART WEIGHT LIMITS: 2340 to 2650 POUNDS
EXTERNAL LOAD ITEMS: NONE

LIMITS	R.P.M.	M.P. (IN. HG.)	BLOWER POSITION	MIXTURE POSITION	TIME LIMIT	TOTAL G.P.H.
WAR MAX						
MILITARY POWER						
NORMAL RATED	2075			F.R.	CONT.	21.3

INSTRUCTIONS FOR USING CHART: Select figure in FUEL column equal to or less than amount of fuel to be used for cruising. Move horizontally to left or right and select RANGE value equal to or greater than the statute or nautical air miles to be flown. Vertically below and opposite desired cruising altitude (ALT.) read optimum R.P.M., I.A.S. and MIXTURE setting required.

NOTES: Column I is for emergency high speed cruising only. Columns II, III, IV and V give progressive increase in range at a sacrifice in speed. Manifold pressure (M. P.), gallons per hour (G. P. H.) and true airspeed (T. A. S.) are approximate values for reference. For efficiency maintain indicated airspeed (I. A. S.) hourly. Adjust RPM slightly if necessary to avoid exceeding manifold pressure more than 3 in. Hg.

I RANGE IN AIR MILES		FUEL U.S. GAL.	II RANGE IN AIR MILES		III RANGE IN AIR MILES		FUEL U.S. GAL.	IV RANGE IN AIR MILES		V RANGE IN AIR MILES	
STATUTE	NAUTICAL		STATUTE	NAUTICAL	STATUTE	NAUTICAL		STATUTE	NAUTICAL	STATUTE	NAUTICAL
220	190	40	240	210	260	225	40	290	250	320	280
190	165	35	210	180	230	200	35	260	225	280	245
160	140	30	180	155	200	175	30	220	190	240	210
135	115	25	150	130	165	145	25	185	160	200	175
110	95	20	120	105	130	115	20	150	130	160	140
80	70	15	90	80	100	85	15	110	95	120	105
55	50	10	60	50	65	55	10	75	65	85	70

MAXIMUM CONTINUOUS — OPERATING DATA

R.P.M.	I.A.S. M.P.H.	MIX. TURE	ALT. Feet	R.P.M.	I.A.S. M.P.H.	MIX. TURE	M.P. In. Hg.	G.P.H.	T.A.S.	R.P.M.	I.A.S. M.P.H.	MIX. TURE	M.P. In. Hg.	G.P.H.	T.A.S.	ALT. Feet	R.P.M.	I.A.S. M.P.H.	MIX. TURE	M.P. In. Hg.	G.P.H.	T.A.S.
			40000													40000						
			35000													35000						
			30000													30000						
			25000													25000						
			20000													20000						
			9000													9000	960	101	P.L.	14.2	15	
			6000													6000	890	102	P.L.	13.6	12	
			3000				2000	115	F.R.			1975	120	F.R.		3000	815	103	F.R.	13.2	08	
2075	127	F.R.	S.L.	21.3	127		3000	115	F.R.	18.3	21	1975	120	F.R.	16.1	18	S.L.	975	108	P.L.			
							S.L.			7.4		1890	114	F.R.	15.8	16		925	111	P.L.			
															15			1890	114	F.R.			

NOTES:
○ Allow 5 GAL. FOR WARM-UP, TAKE-OFF & INITIAL CLIMB PLUS ALLOWANCE FOR WIND, RESERVE & COMBAT AS REQ'D.

EXAMPLE: AT 2650 LB. GROSS WT. WITH 30 GAL. OF FUEL (AFTER DEDUCTING TOTAL ALLOWANCES OF 10 GAL.) TO FLY 240 STAT. AIRMILES AT 9000 FT. ALT. MAINTAIN 1900 RPM 96 MPH IND. AIRSPEED WITH MIXTURE SET P.L.

LEGEND
- I.A.S.: INDICATED AIRSPEED
- M.P.: MANIFOLD PRESSURE
- G.P.H.: U.S. GAL. PER HOUR
- T.A.S.: TRUE AIRSPEED
- S.L.: SEA LEVEL P.L.: PART LEAN
- F.T.: FULL THROTTLE
- F.R.: FULL RICH
- A.R.: AUTO-RICH
- A.L.: AUTO-LEAN
- C.L.: CRUISING LEAN

RED FIGURES ARE PRELIMINARY, SUBJECT TO REVISION AFTER FLIGHT CHECK

Revised 25 May 1944

FLIGHT OPERATION INSTRUCTION CHART

RESTRICTED   T. O. No. 01-115GA-1

MODEL(S): PT-26
ENGINE(S): L-440-3, -7
CHART WEIGHT LIMITS: 2330 TO 2650 POUNDS
EXTERNAL LOAD ITEMS: NONE

LIMITS	R.P.M.	M.P. (IN. HG.)	BLOWER POSITION	MIXTURE POSITION	TIME LIMIT	TOTAL G.P.H.
WAR MAX.						
MILITARY POWER						
NORMAL RATED	2450			F.R.	CONT.	19.3

INSTRUCTIONS FOR USING CHART: Select figure in FUEL column equal to or less than amount of fuel to be used for cruising. Move horizontally to left or right and select RANGE value equal to or greater than the statute or nautical air miles to be flown. Vertically below and opposite desired cruising altitude (ALT.) read optimum R.P.M., I.A.S. and MIXTURE setting required.

NOTES: Column I is for emergency high speed cruising only. Columns II, III, IV and V give progressive increase in range at a sacrifice in speed. Manifold pressure (M.P.), gallons per hour (G.P.H.) and true airspeed (T.A.S.) are approximate values for reference. For efficiency maintain indicated airspeed (I.A.S.) hourly. Adjust RPM slightly if necessary to avoid exceeding manifold pressure more than 3 in. Hg.

I

RANGE IN AIR MILES		FUEL U.S. GAL.
STATUTE	NAUTICAL	
230	200	40
205	180	35
175	150	30
150	130	25
115	100	20
90	80	15
60	50	10

II

RANGE IN AIR MILES		FUEL U.S. GAL.
STATUTE	NAUTICAL	
300	260	40
260	225	35
220	190	30
185	160	25
150	130	20
110	95	15
75	65	10

III

5 GAL. ALLOWANCE NOT AVAILABLE IN FLIGHT

RANGE IN AIR MILES		FUEL U.S. GAL.
STATUTE	NAUTICAL	
320	280	30
280	245	25
245	210	20
205	180	
160	140	15
120	105	
80	70	10

IV

RANGE IN AIR MILES		FUEL U.S. GAL.
STATUTE	NAUTICAL	
350	305	40
305	265	35
265	230	30
220	190	25
175	150	20
130	115	15
85	75	10

V

RANGE IN AIR MILES		FUEL U.S. GAL.
STATUTE	NAUTICAL	
360	315	40
315	275	35
270	235	30
225	195	25
180	155	20
135	115	15
90	80	10

MAXIMUM CONTINUOUS — OPERATING DATA

R.P.M.	I.A.S. M.P.H.	MIX. TURE	M.P. In. Hg.	G.P.H.	T.A.S.	ALT. Feet	R.P.M.	I.A.S.	MIX. TURE	M.P.	G.P.H.	T.A.S.	R.P.M.	I.A.S.	MIX. TURE	M.P.	G.P.H.	T.A.S.	R.P.M.	I.A.S.	MIX. TURE	M.P.	G.P.H.	T.A.S.
						40000																		
						35000																		
						30000																		
						25000																		
						12000	2400	113	P.L.	14.4	124	2400	108	P.L.				2410	104	P.L.	12.2	125	2400	103	P.L.	12.2	124
2400						9000	2360	117	P.L.	14.7	122	2330	111	P.L.	3.4	124	2310	105	P.L.	11.8	120	2290	104	P.L.	11.5	119
2360						6000						2290	113	F.R.	3.1	121	2230	106	P.L.	11.3	116	2210	104	P.L.	10.9	114
2300						3000											2230	108	F.R.	11.2	113	2170	107	F.R.	10.9	112
2450 126 F.R. 19.3 126						S.L.	2300	120	F.R.	14.7	120	2230	116	F.R.	2.9	116	2100	109	F.R.	10.8	109	2065	108	F.R.	10.7	108

MAXIMUM RANGE — OPERATING DATA

NOTES

○ ALLOW 5 GAL. FOR WARM-UP, TAKE-OFF & INITIAL CLIMB PLUS ALLOWANCE FOR WIND, RESERVE & COMBAT AS REQD.

EXAMPLE
AT 2600 LB. GROSS W.T. WITH 35 GAL. OF FUEL (AFTER DEDUCTING TOTAL ALLOWANCES OF 10 GAL.) TO FLY 280 STAT. AIR-MILES AT 9000 FT. ALT. MAINTAIN 2400 RPM AND 108 MPH IND. AIRSPEED WITH MIXTURE SET P.L.

LEGEND

I.A.S.: INDICATED AIRSPEED   F.T.: FULL THROTTLE
M.P.: MANIFOLD PRESSURE   F.R.: FULL RICH
G.P.H.: U.S. GAL. PER HOUR   A.R.: AUTO-RICH
T.A.S.: TRUE AIRSPEED   A.L.: AUTO-LEAN
S.L.: SEA LEVEL   C.L.: CRUISING LEAN
P.L.: PART LEAN
RED FIGURES ARE PRELIMINARY,
SUBJECT TO REVISION AFTER FLIGHT CHECK

Revised 25 May 1944

APPENDIX I

GLOSSARY OF TERMS

American	British
Airplane	Aeroplane
Battery	Accumulator
Carburetor	Carburettor
Empennage	Tail Unit
Engine or Power Plant	Aero Engine
Fairchild PT-19, PT-19A, PT-19B, PT-23, PT-26	Cornell
Fuel Gage	Fuel Contents Gauge
Gas	Petrol or Fuel
Generator	Dynamo
Inverter	Motor Generator
Landing Gear	Alighting Gear
Lean	Weak
Left	Port
Outer Panel	Outer Plane
Pitot	Pressure Head
Right	Starboard
Trim Tab	Trimming Tab
Vent	Vent Pipe
Wing	Main Plane

APPENDIX II
EMERGENCY INSTRUCTIONS

1. **ENGINE FAILURE IN FLIGHT.**

   a. Drop the nose and maintain a gliding speed of 80 mph.

   b. Open cockpit enclosure (PT-26 ONLY).

   c. Ignition switch "OFF."

   d. Make a normal landing if possible.

   e. Master switch "OFF" (PT-19B, PT-23, and PT-26 ONLY).

2. **FIRE.**

   a. PT-26 ONLY. - Do not use the fire extinguisher for fires in flight within the cockpit without first opening the enclosure.

   b. The fire extinguisher door in the forward left fuselage cowl gives easy access to the fire extinguisher mounted on the front portion of the front cockpit. If you are not in the airplane when fire breaks out, with the ship on the ground, use this door to reach the extinguisher.

3. **NOSE-OVER.**

   The turn-over structure on top of the fuselage between the cockpits protects the occupants in the event of nose-over. If the ship should nose over, let yourself down easily with the safety belt or harness. In the PT-26, open the enclosure before landing.

4. **FUEL PUMP FAILURE.**

   Use the hand wobble pump and maintain 2-1/2 to 3-1/2 pound pressure, 2 to 3 pounds on the PT-23.

APPENDIX III
EXTREME WEATHER NOTES

1. **EXTREME COLD.**

   a. Always use oil dilution before stopping engine (PT-26 ONLY).

   b. The use of an electric oil immersion heater is recommended to facilitate starting regardless of whether the airplane is equipped for oil dilution or not.

   c. STARTING.

   (1) Use 3 or 4 shots of primer and 5 or 6 sharp strokes of throttle, 6 or 8 shots of primer only on PT-23.

   (2) Pump throttle rapidly near "CLOSED" position immediately after engine starts to keep it going. (Not applicable to PT-23.)

   (3) Extend warm-up time as long as necessary to assure satisfactory operating before preparing to take off.

   d. CARE OF CONTROLS.

   (1) Keep all controls free from freezing and sticking.

   (2) Lubrication of controls with very light machine oil will help keep them in satisfactory operating condition. Do not lubricate ball bearings.

   e. "Lagging" the oil tank and oil lines with asbestos will help in maintaining satisfactory operating temperatures. This is done by securely wiring sheets of asbestos to the exposed portions of the tank and lines.

   f. Remove all snow, ice, sleet, or slush from every part of the airplane before attempting to take off. Make sure airplane is completely dry and that no moisture remains as this would freeze in flight. Dry snow may be brushed or blown off. Sleet and ice should be very gradually melted off, preferably by the sun or by placing the airplane in a heated hangar and letting it "thaw out" by itself.

   g. Icing conditions occur when flying through rain or clouds when the temperature is approximately freezing or colder. At very cold temperatures or at high altitudes icing is rarely encountered. Do not fly through regions where icing conditions are suspected unless absolutely necessary. If, for some reason, this must be done, watch the leading edges of the wing and tail closely for evidence of ice. Glaze, or clear ice, is the most difficult type to detect. If ice begins to form, land as soon as possible or descend to a lower altitude where the temperature is well above freezing. If there is ice on the wings or tail, land the airplane at somewhat above normal landing speed in order to prevent stalling and to maintain control.

   h. Mooring is sometimes facilitated in cold weather by tying the mooring line around the middle of a large stick or 2 x 4 about 3 feet long and placing it in a hole in the ground about 2 to 3 feet deep. The hole may then be filled with water which will freeze, holding the ship secure. Temperature must be well below freezing if this method is used. Engine and wing covers are recommended to protect the airplane in extreme cold when mooring a ship out-of-doors.

2. **EXTREME HEAT.**

   a. AIR FILTER.

   (1) The only necessary precaution in very hot weather is to inspect the Air Maze filter by removing the screen from the carburetor air intake duct every 7 to 10 hours. Dust and insects might accumulate there to such an extent that satisfactory engine operation might be hampered. The screen may be cleaned by an air pressure hose and nonleaded gasoline.

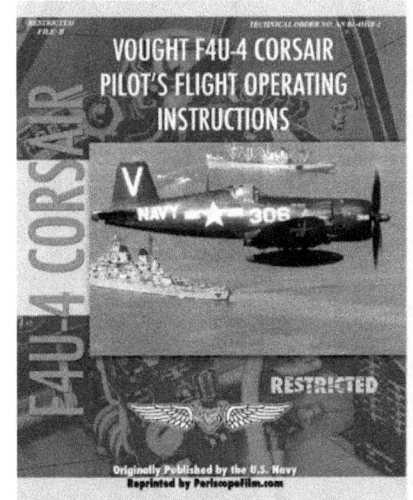
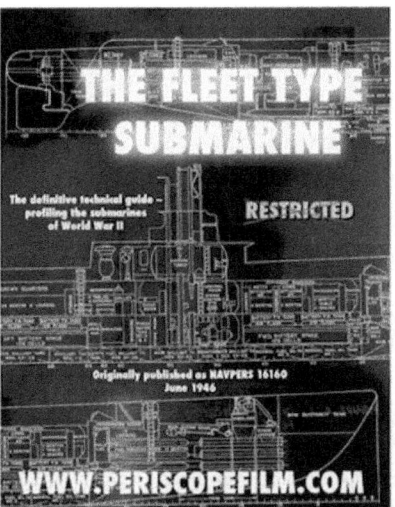
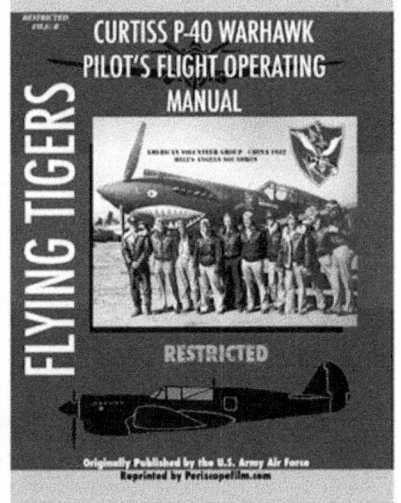

ALSO NOW AVAILABLE FROM PERISCOPEFILM.COM

©2011 PERISCOPE FILM LLC
ALL RIGHTS RESERVED
ISBN# 978-1-935700-57-9

www.ingramcontent.com/pod-product-compliance
Lightning Source LLC
LaVergne TN
LVHW061347060426
835512LV00012B/2596

9781935700579